"These Vibrant Women who opened their hearts & shared their stories serve as an inspiration to men & women everywhere!"
—John Gray, PhD., *Men are from Mars, Women are from Venus* Series

VIBRANT
Women's

WISDOM

SURVIVING AND THRIVING
Through

DARK & BRIGHT HOURS

KELLY PALACE, M.ED.

DR. WANDA BETHEA ✱ LINDA WIGGINS

AND 20 OTHER VIBRANT AUTHORS

FOREWORD BY CAROLINE ADAMS MILLER, MAPP

ISBN-13   978-1-60013-340-4
First Edition

Published by...
INSIGHT PUBLISHING
647 Wall Street
Sevierville, Tennessee 37862

10 9 8 7 6 5 4 3 2 1

This book can be purchased individually or in special quantity discounts (if purchased in bulk) at our website: www.VibrantWomensWisdom.com.

Acknowledgements

Acknowledgement by Kelly Palace, M. Ed.

When I had the idea for this book, it was just that. The encouragement and support from Linda Wiggins and Wanda Bethea helped push me to make it a reality. Thank you, Linda and Wanda, for your enthusiasm, talent, support, love and work. Thank you to all the women authors in this book who stepped forward to tell their stories. I appreciate all of you! I am grateful to my husband Mark (MarkPalace.com), who loves, supports, inspires and motivates me daily. My life has been filled with many dark and bright hours and, thankfully, my entire family has always "doubled my joys and halved my sorrows." I love you Mom and Dad—thank you for your lifelong support, wisdom and love. I must thank all the vibrant women in my life: You all inspire me. And to my two best girlfriends, Beth and Nancy, you are truly vibrant women that I love!

Acknowledgement by Dr. Wanda Bethea

I acknowledge my appreciation to Kelly Palace for offering me this sacred gift! I equally appreciate Linda Wiggins who welcomed me into this project. I also am grateful to my dearest girlfriends DeeLee Bauer and Tracy Heitmann for their love and Beckie Grgich for years of encouragement. I want to thank Linda Pickett and all the other women in my life upon whose shoulders I have stood. I am very appreciative of Dawn Schnuck's willingness to pre-edit my writings. I also am grateful to my young grandchildren, Nathaniel, Kayla and Caira and their giggles. Lastly, to my hero husband, Rick, I am so grateful. You have always been "the wind beneath my wings."

Acknowledgement by Linda Wiggins

I am thankful to God for this opportunity to express my soul gift, and thankful to the human vehicle for allowing herself to be the necessary conduit for that blessing, Kelly Palace. Her divinely-inspired format of favorite quote, passion, darkest hour, lessons from the dark, brightest hour and lesson from the light was the perfect magnet for pulling my gift out of me and the perfect canvas to paint it on. Dr. Wanda Bethea helped me cut through the emotional distractions along my journey through darkness into The Light. I thank and admire my husband Mike for being Mr. Right, and for his willingness to be a role model for other men in my public passion to guide others in their journey toward Being Mrs. Right. I am also thankful for the opportunity to edit the works of these Vibrant women, because in doing so, their insights became my insights, their awareness, mine.

Table of Contents

by Caroline Adams Miller, MAPP

Over twenty years ago, I hit my last bottom with my secret tormenter: bulimia. After seven years of secretly struggling to overcome the deadly binge-purge syndrome, I was in a place where I knew I had a choice between continuing to do what I was doing, which would surely kill me, or reach out for help and start the healing process.

The decision to reach out for help changed my life, and my darkest day became the touchstone for all of my future growth. In fact, the chronicle of my years of bulimia and my recovery became the first major autobiography about recovery from bulimia, *My Name is Caroline* (Doubleday 1988) and it lit the way to recovery for tens of thousands of other people. To this day, that book continues to sell and inspire people to turn their similar dark hours into a springboard back to life, and I'm humbled by the power of that simple book. It gave people hope, which was the equivalent of giving them the keys to the kingdom.

Vibrant Women's Wisdom has the same power to encourage and inspire anyone who picks it up. If you are dealing with divorce, abuse, discrimination, medical issues or any other serious challenge, this book will empower you. Every story has the message that our dark hours are not the end, but that they are, instead, the impetus for resilience and change. We don't always know that is the case when we are surrounded by darkness, but these stories will reassure you that we will emerge stronger, braver and more compassionate specifically because of the darkness.

We never discover our character when life is easy; conversely, it is only through setbacks that we have the need to find out what we are made of. Through crises we gain strength, hope and authentic joy. By developing resilience, we put money in the bank for future crises, and we know we can get through whatever life throws at us. Studies of happy families have even found that the happiest families tell these stories over and over to show future generations that life is about soldiering on and receiving help from others. We become better people when life doesn't always go our way and we have the humility to address it instead of quit.

Treasure this book and turn to it whenever you feel down or overwhelmed. These are stories of triumph and joy, peppered with the nightmarish hours that preceded them, which is what creates the richness that will fill your soul. I am honored to be a part of this tremendous offering to the world, and I trust that many people will be transformed as a result of identifying with the people who have had the courage to share the reality of their lives with us so that we may be inspired and improved.

Caroline Adams Miller, MAPP, Best-selling Author
Creating Your Best Life
My Name is Caroline
Bright Words for Dark Days
Feeding the Soul
www.CarolineMiller.com

Introduction

by Kelly Palace, M.Ed.

This book will reinforce your belief in the strength of the human spirit. It is a journey through 23 Vibrant Women's Dark and Bright hours and the lessons each one learned on the way. There are brave stories, stories that will strengthen and inspire you. You'll be touched by women who overcame, conquered, succeeded, loved, healed, created, beat the odds, lost, grew and shined through! As one saying goes, "truth can be stranger than fiction." You'll laugh, you'll cry, you'll love reading each story.

My vision in creating this book was so that you could reach for it to inspire and strengthen you in times of need. The idea for this book came to me in my darkest hour. What I was going through was so dark and so unjust, I knew I had to write about it when it was over. But I didn't want to do it alone. There is strength in numbers—especially with women. If *my* story needed to be told, I knew there were many others. Gathering these women and their stories for this book was like collecting sea shells on a beach walk. Each one is uniquely beautiful and special.

I created the format for this book so that if you connect with someone's story and would like to, you could reach out to her. This was the idea behind the format for each author to give her: Favorite Quote, Passion, Darkest Hour, Lessons from the Dark, Brightest Hour and Lessons from the Light. Hopefully this format gives a larger glimpse of what each woman is about. We also included each author's contact information in their chapter. These vibrant women agreed to be available to you.

Finally, I invite you to write your own Favorite Quote, Passion, Dark and Bright Hours and Lessons. We have included an activity section in the back of the book with background and guidance on getting the most out of this exercise. We know you will benefit from the experience should you choose to partake.

If you would like to share your story with us, we will be collecting them via our website and would love to read yours. Should we produce another work of this kind we may include you. Please stay in touch with us and follow the book's progress and other Vibrant Women's Wisdom Products at www.VibrantWomensWisdom.com.

It is my hope that by reading this book your life will be more vibrant and you will be strengthened and inspired. Thank you for picking it up.

Chapter One

Leslie Slaasted

Favorite Quote

"You are not what happened to you. You are what you choose to become."— Carl Jung

Passion

I love helping women change their lives by releasing self-limiting behaviors and overcoming emotional, mental, and physical blocks. They then can move toward more fulfillment and create the life they desire, the life they deserve.

Our society offers few venues for women to feel safe, nurtured, understood, supported, and appreciated. My purpose is for every woman I meet to feel the spark of her inner wisdom and divinity glitter and shine. Only by truly supporting one another can we change the world.

Darkest Hour

His suicide note sat four feet inside the front door, centered on the black vinyl keyboard stool. He had moved the stool to the center of the room so I was sure not to miss it.

"I realize no one will understand this decision...."

In that moment, razors shredded every cell of my being into confetti, and my mouth filled with the metallic taste of bile. I forced myself to finish reading his neatly-handwritten note, preparing mind and body for the inevitable. Then with legs filled with concrete, I went to find my fiancé, the revolver still in his right hand, his body beginning to cool.

Always thoughtful, he had positioned himself so I could dole out carefully-measured glances up his body, allowing myself to absorb his death in small doses. I saw his feet first and, when I saw the shirt he had chosen to die in, both love and intense pain pushed at my throat struggling for an outlet. He wore the jeans he had been wearing when we first met along with a velvet, rock-star shirt we had playfully purchased in a vintage shop. His favorite hat lay next to him.

I rested my hands on his chest and sat by his side for several moments wishing and willing him the inner peace he had not been able to find on Earth. I knew that once the police arrived, the early-evening quiet would disintegrate along with my perceptions of the life we had planned. Then I made the phone call.

"My fiancé has committed suicide...."

Swarms of police invaded my yard from all directions, encircling my entire property in yellow crime tape. Neighbors did their best to appear nonchalant in their attempts to look in my windows as they asked the officers what had happened.

I was sequestered inside, prevented from disrupting their investigation. The same questions asked by a dozen different people became a blur, as did the forensics expert who took photographs of every corner of my home, capturing our life, me, and all our belongings on film.

Lastly, the medical examiner took the body of my dearest love away in a black bag, and the flurry of activity suddenly ceased. The yellow crime tape was bundled and thrown in my trash can, and the patrol cars left as quickly as they had arrived. Neighbors whose names I didn't know still paced the sidewalk outside as night took over daylight. I was gut-wrenchingly alone.

My entire being shattered into a thousand glass shards. I frantically clung to all the sharp pieces with bloody hands trying to put them back together, but I couldn't remember what shape they made or how they fit. I had no concept of the new shape my life was supposed to take, so I desperately clutched the shards to my breasts, tendrils of blood dripping down my torso. There was no fixing this.

Lessons from the Dark

Losing my father and my fiancé within three weeks taught me many lessons.

1. No matter what happens in our lives, we can return to wholeness.
2. We must love ourselves. With self-love, all things are possible.
3. It is OK to give fully in love, even if it ends. The human heart loves, hurts, and heals deeply.
4. We can only be responsible for our own actions. We are not responsible for anyone else's feelings or behaviors.
5. It is OK to deeply feel and experience a full range of emotions. They are not dangerous, and by feeling and acknowledging them, we can release them.

Brightest Hour

I pulled the anchor up hand over hand in the small harbor in Wrightsville Beach, N.C. With each ray of luminous, pink-orange light from the rising sun, the abusive relationship I had left back in Maryland seemed more and more distant.

The water lapped gently at my hull as my bow swung free. I pulled the remaining chain and anchor up on deck and secured it as my sailboat drifted in the mild current.

I walked back to the cockpit and put the boat in gear. I was captain of my little ship. My crew consisted of two border collies and three cats. So far, I had singlehanded almost 2,000 miles up and down the coast. This was my first ocean journey.

I inhaled deeply, smelling the sea air on the other side of the barrier island. It was just a short distance to the inlet. My dogs, Allie and Dana, stood on the seats of the cockpit. They sensed my anticipation and eagerly stared forward, noses twitching at the new scents. I double-checked to make sure their harnesses were tied fast to the boat and that they had enough room to move around in the cockpit.

I turned the large wheel to the left and maneuvered my sailboat into the inlet. I felt a surge of energy as the keel of my boat caught the current and increased the throttle to maintain steerage.

I cleared the last buoy and set my compass heading south. I wriggled into my harness and clipped myself securely to the safety cables to move forward and raise the mainsail. The sailcloth crackled as the large winch cranked it higher and higher. I carefully slid my way back to the cockpit, turned the boat back into the wind, and unfurled the forward sail.

The boat naturally fell off the wind, and I adjusted my lines so the sails balanced. Once I was confident the sails were set, I shut off the diesel. As the heavy engine rumbled to a stop, a steady whoosh and gentle splash of water became the only audible sounds as we headed to Charleston, S.C.

My depth sounder told me I was in 98 feet of water, and a sliver of nervousness jolted through my body. I was out of sight of land with nothing around me and would spend the next 24 hours at sea in my small sailboat.

I briefly considered turning back. Then I forced myself to look up at the beauty of the sails against the sky and closed my eyes to embody the rhythmic undulations of the ocean. With eyes closed, I felt the healing pulses and whispers of all the grandmothers who had come before me.

I opened my eyes, full of peace. As I let go of any remaining fear, my heart overflowed with gratitude. I was alive, I was traveling our womblike ocean, and I would never again be hurt by the hands of a man.

Lessons from the Light

1. We have the ability and power to do anything. Our self-imposed limitations keep us small.
2. It is more important to be able to meet our own eyes in a mirror and say, "I love you," than anything else.
3. Inner peace is worth the work to achieve and maintain it.
4. A single, significant accomplishment can overcome any injury to our body/mind/spirit if we allow ourselves to heal and grow.
5. We have a responsibility to live LARGE. Living small hurts us and everyone else we meet.

Biography

Leslie Slaasted is a speaker, writer, master hypnotherapist, certified life coach and wellness coach, and ordained minister. Her company, Insight Solutions, LLC, offers hypnotherapy and meditation CDs, e-books and workbooks, personal growth coaching, spiritual counseling and hypnotherapy.

Leslie also offers a Women's Sanctuary, providing women with a safe and magical place to share and explore camaraderie, personal growth, spiritual development, workshops, peacefulness, art, music, healing food, support, nurturing, and enhanced well-being. Subscribers receive monthly gifts, downloadable files, and access to The Sanctuary. To receive the monthly newsletter, please email leslie@insightsolutionswellness.com.

Leslie Slaasted

Insight Solutions, LLC & The Sanctuary
561-634-6443
www.LeslieSlaasted.com
Leslie@LeslieSlaasted.com

Chapter Two

Joan Sofet

Favorite Quote

"If I rise on the wings of the dawn,
if I settle on the far side of the sea,
even there your hand will guide me,
your right hand will hold me fast."
—Psalm 139: 9-10

Passion

My passion is LOVING! It's my hobby. I go out of my way to love. I love people through encouragement and hugs. I'll love a passerby with a compliment on a pretty outfit. Seniors get my love in homemade soup and phone calls. I show a stranger love by giving a smile. Sad friends are loved with silliness or hilarious ideas of blatant verbal revenge toward whoever's slighted them. I love my friend Leslie with tiny gifts of things that are purple. I can love without jealousy or suffocation. I aspire to love those who wish me harm. My goal is to love everyone. LOOK OUT! I want to love *you*, *too!*

Darkest Hour

Even though I lived on the sixth floor, I KNEW I had intruders. The people on my balcony were really lively that night. I wasn't sure if they were the police, or possibly some savage criminals. I remember peeping – half-crazed and extremely terrified – through the blinds, but the people eluded me once again. I walked through the apartment turning on every light and searching behind every door, in every closet, to make sure they hadn't gotten in. I looked out the peephole until it hurt. Then I came down. My heart stopped pounding and so I walked throughout my home, closing doors and turning off lights – and then I took another hit. The next nine hours were an exact replay. It was only 1997; I had barely gotten started, but at the age of 37, I had become a crack addict.

The story of my trip into darkness – from which most addicts don't return – could be told as simply as: "*There was this guy*," and many women would nod, knowingly. He knew the fast way down the toilet and I followed. His standard of comfort was always a few levels below mine, so he was perfectly fine when I began to tap out all my resources.

My IRA? I smoked it. Credit? Maxed. The stocks? Smoked them, too. I was a professional graphic designer, living comfortably making $65,000 a year. Then came the classic progression of nearly every crack-addicted professional.... Losses! Big losses! First you lose the job, for being unreliable (because you can't always make it into work after hitting a crack pipe until dawn). Next you lose the house, the car. Then, whatever's left. After that, you just LOSE.

Many people can't "get" someone else's plight by simply hearing a story. I mean, regarding my habit, some would say, "HOW could you DO that?! Why not just stop?" Believe me. It was a nightmare. I was so STUCK. Serious drug addiction puts you under its "spell" and you can't *just stop*; even if you don't want to use, you *want* to use.

I looked for people who had quit and completely stayed away from it. In five years, I found only *one*. To even better understand, read this next part slowly. Crack cocaine usually makes people have a strong urge to *defecate* when impending usage is imminent. Get this: When you're about to use, when it's in your hand, still in the plastic bag – before it's even touching your skin – you have to *crap*. If you had a tail it would *wag* uncontrollably. The stuff is evil; it's *devilish*.

I'm convinced that the only way a human can battle that kind of evil is with God. That is when I learned to pray.

Lessons from the Dark

I believe we are "wired' to be close to our Creator. I believe God uses times of great despair to draw us closer to Him. I want to say that on my trip down the toilet, I went willingly. In the long journey back to being a citizen, I found out I hated my life. I found out I was responsible for my own actions. I found real people who showed me love, many of them, fellow Christians. I finally found GOD. I've been saved from the darkness!

Statistically, "the darkness" calls most addicts back. One must remain vigilant and steadfast against any thought of using. I've not used in seven years and I don't dare repeat that history again. I don't *dare* disrespect the hold that crack has and will always have on some subliminal level. To forget is to relapse. You must *always respect* the fact that once you're a member of that club, you're *never* not a club member again. But that doesn't mean you have to attend the meetings. Thank God! Of course, this may mean a person will have to join a *different* club, or group, and seek other kinds of meetings to fill the space of those abandoned. While the 12 Steps was not my final answer to recovery, I believe it is important to continually take steps toward The Light.

Brightest Hour

I was always capable of keeping my household going, or throwing a meal together for myself, but didn't often take time to cook, or shop, or do much of *anything* on a "regular" schedule. I didn't have to. Wheee!! Not even a *plant* relied on me for its survival and I fully enjoyed that degree of freedom.

One day, however, my life changed drastically and I have never been the same. The best time in my life was the several months when I became my parents' caregiver.

My relationship with my folks had not always been the best, and I often prayed that the "family dynamic" would improve. I prayed about it – really hard – for months. I did *not* see it as an answer to prayer when my father unexpectedly wound up in the hospital, but it turned out to be a catalyst for some major healing in our relationship.

Mama was my companion for the next few weeks as I stayed with her while Dad was away. I really enjoyed spending that time with my mom – although being away from Dad was hard on her. It was terribly hard on them both. They had been married for over 60 years at that point. Their completely "symbiotic" relationship was understandable. Mom and I tried to make the best of the circumstances.

We'd have a nice visit with Dad every day, and then I'd make something good for dinner or Mom would buy us a salad. Afterward, I'd construct a fabulous dessert and we'd watch the classic movie channel. Sometimes we'd just talk and I'd learn about my grandmother, or my mom's childhood, or mine, or about my grandfather, who could pick up any instrument and play it. I loved that. The next day we'd start again.

Thankfully, Dad's condition seemed to be improving, and he was finally allowed to come home. He was better, but was not fully recovered. Running the household, with all its little chores and duties, was pretty much My Thing while he was gone, and I continued to do as much as he would "allow" when he came back. My father had to be reminded Not to Do Everything because he sure attempted it! As frustrating as it was for him, Dad was very "cool" about relinquishing some tasks, simply because it was in the best interests of his health and wellbeing. After a while we settled into a nice rhythm of the errands, meals and appointments that made up each week. My Dad and I became true friends during that time, and I'll always treasure the memory of it.

Weeks went by, then months. My apartment had become just a place that I would occasionally "wave to" and grab clothing from. Doing business was a "trip" as well. It's amazing what one can quickly learn to live without! I had been networking and attempting to build up my client base. Soon, though – barring a few select projects – all of it went by the wayside. My life was on hold until my parents moved away. I knew that I was exactly where I was supposed to be.

God gave me the chance to spend quality time with both my parents before they relocated to an out-of-state retirement community. The plan was already in place for them to live near my brothers' families. I helped ready them for their big move while trying not to think of them going away.

Yes, it was one of the hardest things I've ever done. Yes, I exceeded what I thought were my limitations. Yes, I was an artist one month and then impersonating a nurse the next. (I didn't know I could do that!) And, yes, I would do it all again in a heartbeat!

Lessons from the Light

Standing in my parents' driveway as they pulled away, I was numb to the despair I would feel (for weeks) over "losing them." Some referred to it as "empty nest syndrome." It took about a week for it to kick in, and then I cried every time I thought about them - every day. I stopped wanting to get up. I had lost my purpose. I didn't want to do anything at all. I began to generally loathe humanity. I didn't like what I began to see in me. (Especially evident in traffic!) With the help of a few caring friends, my good sister, and my spiritual advisors, I worked very hard to figure it out.

What I realized: The bitterness of "unforgiveness" was totally jamming me up! I partly cried it out and partly prayed and thought it out, but the bottom line was that even if I was a loving caregiver for someone else, I didn't show that same loving care for myself. I was not allowing God's unending, unconditional LOVE and forgiveness for myself into my own heart. I was also not allowing the love and affection from other humans to *really register* when I would receive it. I realized I had to make a *conscious effort* to remember the real hugs and warmth of my *own* "caregivers."

Caregivers are everywhere - in restaurants, pharmacies, doctor offices - I just didn't "see" them until I became one. Pay attention; they're there.

Biography

Native to the Washington, D.C. area, but now a resident of Florida, Joan has worked as a graphic design artist since before computers. She enjoys creating works of art for her clients and volunteering at her church, St. Mark's United Methodist Church in Indialantic, Fla. She helps fellow members discover their spiritual gifts; mentors women just released from incarceration; serves on the church communications team; designs, decorates, face-paints, and sometimes uses Play-Doh and crayons with the kids in the nursery.

"I believe that we're here to love and help each other," says Joan, "and to try and move closer and closer to 'sainthood.'" Still, she admits, "It's not always easy, but definitely something to aspire to."

Joan Sofet

VisualJones@yahoo.com
www.MyVisualJones.com
321-956-9567

Chapter Three

Dr. Wanda Bethea

Favorite Quote

> "I cried because I did not have enough of something else.
> Then the sun came out and touched my face.
> I made a laughing bowl to catch the tears
> To bathe the hands that touched me."—Sioux Indian Epigram

My art teacher sent me this "condolence" when my mother died. I have used it many times since.

Passion

I love helping others, especially children and adolescents, to understand that no matter how bleak things may appear, a rainbow lies just around the corner. I am fulfilling my passion when I can encourage them to hold on until tomorrow, even if circumstances make them feel all alone. I want people to believe that as long as they are still standing, marvelous things are possible.

I welcome public speaking opportunities that allow me to promote the character strengths of gratitude, wisdom, humanity, curiosity, knowledge, love, awe, courage, emotional intelligence, forgiveness, and justice—all of which are essential, I believe, for authentic happiness.

Darkest Hour

Each Friday after school, my mother and I would grocery shop together. One rainy Friday, 20 days before my 18th birthday, I went shopping as usual with Mommy. I behaved very badly while we shopped, whining and demanding that she buy me a bag of Spanish peanuts. She refused.

When we had finished, I dropped her off at the hair salon. I was still angry. About an hour later, the telephone rang. My mother had been taken to the hospital—and died.

I was furious with the doctor who had overmedicated my mom for her high blood pressure for so many years. I hated the nurses at the hospital who left her alone and unattended in a small dark room while they laughed and smirked about Cassius Clay changing his name. They had been so preoccupied with their nonsense that they neglected to put blankets on my mother's bed. I distrusted and disrespected the medical community for years after my mother's death. I was disappointed and angry with God. I felt suicidal. I would spend subsequent years in college as a self-proclaimed agnostic and borderline atheist.

I could not believe that my nurturer, angel, and cheerleader mother would not be with me to celebrate my birthday or my high school graduation. She would not help me pack for my first year of college—or, later, see me marry or hold my son at birth. *My soul was empty and I was lost.*

She had been the first to identify and support my creativity. She made sure that I had iridescent paints, drawing paper, pipe cleaners, crayons and coloring books to inspire my self-expression, as well as the *Nancy Drew* series to foster my curiosity. With her encouragement, I played Mozart when I was 7 years old. At 10, I traveled by commuter train into New York City to take weekly singing lessons. I sang in the same *CBS* building as child star Connie Francis and opera singer Beverly Sills. My mom loved to hear me sing *"When you walk through a storm hold your head up high . . ."*

Both my parents sacrificed to create opportunities for me to shine, but it was my mom who taught me the importance of courage and self-respect. When someone jumped in front of her as she waited in line, she quickly gave them fierce eye contact. That individual knew unequivocally that she would not tolerate their lack of consideration. She was a 5'3" fireball and only one thing incapacitated her indomitable spirit. That was my father's manly indifference.

My mom did not believe in being a "friend" to her daughter. She had no patience for my being fresh. She had zero tolerance for back talk even though occasionally I muttered something unkind under my breath—as I did about those Spanish peanuts on that fateful Friday. Since her death, 44 long years ago, I have never wanted another Spanish peanut. *Oh, Mommy, can you forgive me? I am so sorry.*

Lessons from the Dark

I have learned to honor each and every minute because things can change in the "twinkling of an eye." I understand that I must keep on pushing, no matter what challenges confront me. I work to be more understanding of human foibles and vulnerabilities. I make it a habit to speak my mind and heart as needed. I create sacred spaces to foster my personal peace and purpose. And, as the song goes, *"I believe for every drop of rain that falls, a flower grows . . . I believe that somewhere in the darkest night, a candle glows."*

Brightest Hour

My father's decision to allow me to spend my sophomore year of college studying abroad was truly my brightest hour. At first, he was reluctant to let his only child fly off to Europe alone, but my paternal grandmother was a strong supporter of her grandchild's cultural enrichment. Since my dad always conferred with his mother about important matters, my European trip became a reality.

And so it happened that I studied art, music, and history in France, Germany, and Spain. It was glorious to roam the well-known Left Bank in France, to stroll the walkways along the Seine River, and to marvel at the elegance of the Eiffel Tower. I found Heidelberg to be avant-garde and Mainz quaint. I must say that figures in black-face on floats in local parades gave me pause.

I discovered that the students in Spain were intellectual and fiercely spirited about their government. They also taught me the significance of siestas and offered good reasons for women to avoid shaving their legs.

My studies included trips to the Louvre, important cathedrals, and other famous cities throughout the Continent. During semester breaks, I vacationed in Amsterdam, Holland; Copenhagen, Denmark; and Tangiers, Morocco. Everywhere I traveled, people happily gave me help and treated me with kindness.

I took some risks. As a young woman in 1967 I backpacked alone in several exotic and dangerous cities. One man tried to rape me while I rode in a train car. Apart from that, many others protected me.

A young German took me into his home when I missed curfew and was locked out of the youth hostel where I was staying. Earlier that evening, he talked to me about how upset and sad he felt that people thought all Germans were like Hitler. That night, I slept safely in one of his beds, covered with a down feather comforter.

Several Moroccan men with whom I drank mint tea in the *casbah* warned me about traveling to Marrakech, a city I really wanted to visit. They described in graphic detail the dangers awaiting a single woman, especially an unveiled foreign one, in northern Africa.

A young Spanish soldier I met on a train spoke passionately about President Franco's mission and reign. He taught me a great deal about dictatorships and I fell in love with the compassion in this soldier's dark eyes as he talked about his experiences.

Ah, and then I met an attractive black Dutch man in Holland. We rode bikes at all hours of the night, exploring the beauty of Amsterdam's famous flower gardens.

My father was right to be concerned about my travels. He knew that my adventurous spirit occasionally led me into careless risk-taking. When I returned to America, he was very relieved that I arrived home alive and well. It was wonderful to tell him about my adventures, especially about the people I met. They were the real treasures I found abroad—and they couldn't fit inside my backpack. How grateful I was for the experience.

Lessons from the Light

I believe multicultural differences and similarities should be honored and explored by families, and in schools and communities. An adventurous spirit creates incredible opportunities and wonderful memories. Knowledge of and love for humanity encourages respect for others. Young girls blossom in the development of their curiosity and courage. Sometimes one must *"walk in the direction of the cannons."*

Biography

Dr. Wanda Bethea is a licensed psychologist, personal and executive coach, public speaker and adjunct professor. She is committed to promoting Positive Psychology principles in her work with children, adolescents, families, couples and organizations. She believes deeply in the power of the character strengths of wisdom, zest, love of humanity, justice, gratitude, courage, emotional intelligence, awe, and spirituality to increase peak performance for her clients.

Dr. Wanda Bethea

www.drbethea.com
drbethea@cfl.rr.com
321- 724-6177 (office)

Chapter Four

Christel Milak-Parker, M. Ed.

Favorite Quote

"What lies behind us and what lies before us are tiny matters compared to what lies within us."—Ralph Waldo Emerson

Passion

I love to travel, especially with my husband, Steve. We enjoy exploring new places both near and far. Although I am no longer the daredevil of my youth, skiing is still one of my favorite pastimes. Spending time in the company of people who are funny, positive and inspiring energizes me. I want to follow my heart, seek new knowledge, pursue adventure and bond closer with those I love – both family and friends. Ideally, I want to inspire others through genuineness.

Darkest Hour

When Michael and I exchanged our wedding vows at the ages of 28 and 25 respectively, when we said the words "'til death do us part," the reality that death would part us in 10 years could not have been further from our minds. Our plan was to grow old together.

"You have cancer" said the doctor. The doctor's words confirmed my inner dread that something was terribly wrong with my husband. I was terrified. Michael already looked like a shadow of his former, healthy self. Michael's doctor told us that he wanted to admit Michael to the hospital so the biopsy could be performed the next day. My husband and protector replied, "You just told my wife that I have cancer. I am not sending her home alone tonight." The diagnosis of pancreatic cancer was a death sentence – three months to the date, Michael died. Our daughter Megan had just turned 8 and our son Jeff would turn 5 just 10 days later. I was a widow and single parent at 35.

Initially I felt only despair and numbness. Despair sucks, especially when it seems indefinite. Numbness was my relief from despair, a stupor devoid of emotions – I felt more like a robot than a person. "Who am I now?" was the persistent and haunting question I posed to myself. I used to be optimistic, energetic and fun. Michael had referred to me as a committee waiting to happen because of my drive and enthusiasm for community service. Now I was tired, forgetful, frustrated and sad. My abnormality was acceptable considering the circumstances, but how long would this last?

Grieving is painful work. Meg and Jeff were the reason I dragged myself out of bed each day and attempted a normal routine. Michael's absence was ever present, so normal was not realistic. My children were angry and, when not too numb or exhausted, so was I. I read books and went to support groups because Meg and Jeff's recovery was dependent on mine. My quest for knowledge and understanding revealed a heartbreaking truth. Due to their young age, Meg and Jeff would remember very little about their father. Michael once told me that one of the best things about living in the South was that when Meg was an adult, she would still call him "Daddy." Now Daddy would consist of isolated memories, old photographs and other people's stories when my children became adults. Their loss was far greater than mine.

I became the target for my children's anger. With the best of intentions, I would plan a trip or special event for the three of us so we could enjoy quality time together. Often, my efforts were not appreciated. Meg and Jeff would willingly jump into the car and either on the way there or once we arrived, they would begin arguing and fighting, not only with each other, but also with me. I was both angered and embarrassed by their behavior. They were hateful toward me and each other.

My darkest hour was at the end of a disastrous day, when I would wonder whether Michael's fate was the lesser of two evils. I did not wish for death; however, in these moments, life seemed the more burdensome of the two.

Lessons from the Dark

People are unbelievably kind. I never lacked support but I did have to learn to ask for help when I needed it. There is a significant difference between understanding and accepting my limitations and failure; vulnerability is not synonymous with weakness. Healing takes time and patience, not only with myself but with others as well. My children felt safe enough with me to spill their anguish. My friends can cry with me as easily as they can laugh with me. Annoyance over petty inconveniences is still petty, but also a positive sign, as it indicates a return to the "real world." Laughter is truly medicinal.

Brightest Hour

Epiphanies are not part of my biography; my personal journeys are what best define my "brightness." As a result of my new ventures, both personal and professional, I can joyously declare that I have my life back – living, loving and laughing are again my reality.

I am blessed to have married another wonderful man, Steve. He is my lover, partner and best friend. Our marriage began with blended family struggles – five teenagers under one roof! Our relationship persevered and we just celebrated our 10th anniversary. We now enjoy our "empty nest" (with the exception of our two dogs). Our children are now young adults, either in college or finished with their schooling for now. It is liberating to know that, yes, we made mistakes as all parents do, but our decisions, often difficult ones, were made with our children's well-being as the first consideration.

I started my own business eight years ago. Entrepreneurship suits my creative and independent nature. I still work on running the business versus having it run me at times, but I do like looking in the mirror to ask the boss if I can have a week or two off, and seeing her smile and reply, "Sure, you've earned it!" The greatest benefit for me as a business owner is the ability to direct and structure my business so earning money (notice I did not use the verb working) is something I truly enjoy.

I vividly remember the first time one of my clients said, "I told my friend to call you because you are the expert." Since then, I have been referred to as an expert many times, not only by my clients but also by my professional colleagues. It is very affirming to be recognized as an expert in my field. Yes, this is in part due to my knowledge and competence, but the most significant contribution to my expertise is acknowledging the areas where I am not an expert, either due to a lack of experience or by choice. I find it empowering to decide where I do and do not want to acquire expertise.

It is the end of my work day. I have enjoyed some "girlfriend time," either in person or by phone, and met with a number of clients. At the end of our meeting, my clients are less stressed and more confident because I have left them with a plan and/or helped them complete a task. I have some new, prospective business ventures to investigate. Arriving home, I am greeted by two wagging tails and my husband's strong, warm embrace. The feeling is euphoria – not unusual, but dazzlingly bright.

Lessons from the Light

Competence and professionalism are not the result of my knowledge, as much as my ability to communicate with others to the point of understanding. What I hear is far more important than my spoken words. I have learned more from my mistakes than my victories. I derive deep, personal satisfaction from helping others solve a problem or crisis. Pursuing a passion requires effort but it is not work. Personal growth and satisfaction are the result of having the faith to take a risk. Success and happiness are exponential when shared with someone.

Biography

Christel Milak-Parker, M.Ed. is an independent college consultant/planner and the founder of College Connections. College Connections advocates a proactive approach to college planning. She lives in Midlothian, Virginia with her husband, Steve. Christel's business background, prior to education, was in human resources and marketing communications.

Christel Milak-Parker, M.Ed.

christel@collegeconnections.net
(804) 379-8538
www.collegeconnections.net

Chapter Five

Dr. Melissa Andersson

Favorite Quote

"Believe. No pessimist ever discovered the secret of the stars or sailed an uncharted land, or opened a new doorway for the human spirit."—Helen Keller

Passion

To live in the field of quantum possibilities, to take people to new levels of all that they can be – that's my passion. My even greater passion is to lift the circle of life higher through love and abundance. When people are more abundant and "switched on" to the wonders that they possess inside, they are more able to produce results and give more to the world around them.

Darkest Hour

No, this can't be! Not in this country. Please God let me wake up. This has to be a nightmare.

I didn't know at the time that I was to become a small part of a "bigger picture." I didn't know that my convictions about hope, courage, love, transformation and vibrant living would be born out my darkest hours.

Growing up in a small town nestled in the Maryland mountains, I knew nothing of prejudice or hate. At 9 years old, when my parents divorced, my Mom and I moved to Selma, Alabama – just weeks after the infamous "Bloody Sunday."

Until that time, my "world view" was that we are all God's children – no matter our color or gender – and that each of us deserve love and respect. It was 1965, a dark time in the Deep South, and people were murdered just for being "colored" – the term in those days for African Americans. White people were brutalized or killed as well for trying to help them.

Dr. Martin Luther King, Jr. and many other heroes of humanity were fighting peacefully for human rights, human dignity and for the right for black people to vote in the South without harassment.

I grew up with the concept that we live in a democracy where every man, woman and child has a right to engage in respectful communication for the greater good of all. Beginning at age 9, that concept nearly cost me my life.

In school I wrote essays about human rights. Some teachers – in front of the class – demoralized me and led the way for me to have my life threatened. Several times, kids from those classes threatened me with knives. Their words still resonate in my mind, "You keep your mouth shut or you ain't gonna be able to say nothing no more", "You Yanks better stay outta here or there's gonna be more of you killed."

"Bloody Sunday" horrified the world when video documenting the attacks was broadcast on the news. The violent attacks where ordered by the Alabama governor and carried out by state troopers, the Selma sheriff and men on foot and horseback. The victims were men, women and children gathering peacefully to protest for human rights and freedom. They were tear-gassed, trampled and beaten bloody with whips and clubs.

Dr. King and other compassionate leaders organized another march from Selma to Montgomery. Courageous people, of every color, from all over the world, risked their lives to join the march and stand united for humanity. President Johnson ordered troops to protect them. After this historic event, the Voting Rights Act was put in place.

Unfortunately, after the troops left and the media cameras pointed elsewhere, the brutality did not end. Soon after, I watched a peaceful gathering of African Americans in celebration. Their joy was contagious.

Their love for each other was obvious. Then came men with broken beer bottles. People said they were the Sheriff's men and Ku Klux Klan members. They went after a tiny little girl, just about my size. I had been watching her big brown eyes – so full of hope and possibility. I wanted to know her and share in her hopes, her dreams and her passions. And then...in a moment... I saw those beautiful brown eyes turn to terror.

All logical thought left me. I rushed toward the little girl. It was a black man – the little girl's father – who protected me. He stood between me and the violent men. I ended up on the ground, bruised and terrified but safe. Unfortunately, the young father did not succeed in protecting his daughter. I watched the men slash the little girl. I watched the blood pour from her beautiful little face. Her daddy and mommy, so loving and protective, could not help her.

I did not know how to find the purpose and meaning in violence, bigotry and hate. I did not yet know how to understand why some human beings need to dominate others. As a sensitive and compassionate child I entered "the dark night of my soul."

Lessons from the Dark

Sometimes our darkest hours lead us to seek the greatest light. I started my ninth year of life surrounded by mentors, teachers and loved ones. Suddenly I was virtually alone in a world I didn't understand. I clung to the hope that somehow I could figure out how to heal the despair and hopelessness that was consuming me. It took every ounce of my strength to reach for possibilities.

After the divorce – even though Mom worked two jobs, day and night – we barely had enough money to survive. However, I owned one thing which was valuable beyond measure. It was a library card – and it was free. It was my lifeline. I learned from psychologists, sociologists, spiritual teachers and great leaders. I got inspiration from the biographies of people who'd faced great challenges and gone on to make great contributions to humanity.

Brightest Hour

My brightest hours came from "Angels" in human form.

Mom and I had moved to Montgomery hoping for a better life. However, when I was 11 years old things got worse for me. I'd worked hard to heal myself and grow my strength and inner spirit. Yet, there came authoritative forces which seemed intent on dehumanizing me and killing my spirit. I experienced sexual bigotry like never before.

I look back with the awareness that I was suffering from Post Traumatic Stress Disorder (PTSD) and severe depression. No one seemed to acknowledge the "deer in headlights" look in my eyes or the signs of a child in emotional hell. But Miss Nellie did.

Miss Nellie was a cook, a "colored" person, from the school lunch line. She reached for my hand and led me to the kitchen. She gathered me up in her arms against her ample body and she held me.

She said, "Baby Girl, I don't know what you are going through but I know that God doesn't give you anything that you can't handle. I know God loves you and if He's given you a heavy load He sees a purpose in you, a greater purpose that you may not know about right now." She added, "Don't let anybody or anything hold you back from your God-given light." She encouraged my tears to flow.

After that day, we moved away and I never saw Miss Nellie again. However, to me, she continues to be an angel that God sent in human form.

Some years ago I was flying cross country to facilitate a seminar in Las Vegas on human potential, healing, joy and triumph of the human spirit. I thought of Miss Nellie and those few moments of safety, unconditional love, encouragement and compassion. They gave courage to a little girl who pondered that death could be the only escape from her pain. Those moments shaped the work that I do today.

From Orlando to Las Vegas tears flowed down my face. This time, they were tears of gratitude. For a while I fell asleep and Miss Nellie appeared in a dream. She said, "Hey Baby Girl, you know now why God called you to Alabama at that time don't you? He needed legions of light...and you were part of the plan."

I thought of all that transpired during my time in Alabama and the social progress since then. I remembered all the many "angels" who showed up in my life. There were many, many people who where good, loving, decent and kind. Many people really cared greatly for humanity and they wanted the positive change that was emerging. More and more they became part of the change. More and more they came into my life. We formed networks of "light workers."

I remembered the scary times, like when I stood up for blacks to be taught black history in school and the police held guns to my head.

I remembered our wonderful networks of teenagers and adults when I volunteered to help teenagers who'd been abused – emotionally, physically or sexually. I held them in my arms while they cried in emotional release of the horrors they'd endured. They were finally safe and our little "underground railroad" of connections worked to provide them with what they needed next.

I remembered my fear of the responsibility when I was asked to be a peer group suicide counselor at age 16. Then I learned that the key was to get out of my head and into my heart and it wasn't so scary after all.

I let myself acknowledge the "Circle of Life." Probably there are people alive today who turned their pain into humanitarian passion and are touching lives in unimaginable ways, in part because I stepped up for them, just like Miss Nellie and others did for me.

I started work on cruise ships at age 22 and traveled the world. Yet it was our "sea of humanity" which brought me the deepest joy. We were people working together from countless cultures and countries. We were like a mini United Nations. With willingness, familiarity, cooperation and respect it's not so difficult for people to love each other.

Lessons from the Light

Today, as I write this, we are celebrating Dr. Martin Luther King, Jr.'s birthday as a national holiday. Tomorrow we witness the historic presidential inauguration of Barack Obama. In 1963, Dr. King said in a speech, "I have a dream that my four children will one day live in a nation where they will not be judged by the color of their skin but by the content of their character." We have come a long way. Alone we can do so little. Together we can do so much.

Biography

Dr. Melissa Andersson is a Positive Breakthrough Specialist, Peak Performance Trainer and International Speaker. She is co-author of "The Law of Business Attraction; Secrets of Cooperative Success." She is a Doctor of Natural Medicine, a Certified Mental Health Traumatologist, a Certified Pastoral Counselor, a Certified Firewalk Instructor and a specialist in Stress Relief, Kinesiology and Energy Psychology. In 2003 she received a "Humanitarian of the Year" award for her volunteer work around the world. She is the creator of the "Awaken Your Inner Awesome TM Seminars and Retreats," which take people on a journey of the "Human Possible," laughing, joyous and in awe of their capacities.

Dr. Melissa Andersson

HumanPotentialCentral.com
321-631-4JOY
DrMelissa@HumanPotentialCentral.com

Chapter Six

Marjorie Beckett

Favorite Quote

"The Truth Shall Set You Free."—John 8:32

Passion

My life's passion is to work with women of all ages to help them to believe in themselves, motivate them to pursue their dreams and encourage them to achieve their goals. Promoting financial awareness among all people is another passion. Women, especially, need to be financially aware due to their changing circumstances, lower pay, smaller retirement benefits and longer life span than men.

Darkest Hour

I have actually had two darkest hours in my lifetime. The first was when my father died of Hodgkin's disease when I was 9 years old. Prior to his death, I was a very happy child, full of life and love for everyone and everything. Soon after my father died, we moved from New Jersey to Fort Lauderdale, Fla. leaving all of our family and friends behind. At first, moving seemed so exciting, but then reality hit along with the realization that our father was no longer with us. Family and friends were miles and miles away. It all began to sink in. Growing up is hard enough, but when you encounter such devastating circumstances at such a young age, it makes it very difficult to process life and to trust that things are going to be OK.

The second darkest hour was when my husband of eight years went to work one day and never came home. What followed was nothing short of a nightmare. It all began with the filing of a missing person's report which resulted in a search and then lead me to having to take a lie detector test to prove my innocence. I was nervous and scared that something could go wrong and that my children would suffer the consequences. It made me sick to my stomach. I was told that there is a list of about 500 things that they look for (i.e. fabricating a story to get on welfare, killing a spouse to get life insurance money) when investigating such cases and that it would be in my best interest to take the lie detector test. Even my three small children, ages 3, 5 and 7, were questioned about the whereabouts of their father.

In the days that followed, I felt so alone. I remember sitting with my daughters on the park bench outside of the police station, feeling lost and confused, wondering what I was going to do. I was just devastated. You see, I had no idea what happened to my husband, whether he was dead or alive. Then one evening when I was reading my Bible, I found the verse that says, "The truth shall set you free." I clung to that verse like a life preserver. I also came upon a 24-inch by 20-inch poster of the *Footprints* poem which I hung in my living room as a daily reminder of how the Lord was with me and cared about me.

To this day, I still love the last paragraph of that poem. "The Lord replied, 'My precious child, I love you and would never leave you. During your time of trial and suffering, when you see only one set of footprints, it was then that I carried you.'"

Four months to the date of his disappearance, my husband made contact with an old friend, so the case was dropped. He was noted as a "runaway dad." I learned that the statistics are high for runaway moms and dads and that they usually make contact within four months. I was told an active search doesn't even start until after the four months.

Lessons from the Dark

No matter how devastating a situation you find yourself in, if you have faith, believe in yourself, continue doing what you know is right and do what you are supposed to be doing, everything will work out. For "We know that God causes all things to work together for good to those who love God and are called according to His purpose." Romans 8:28.

Brightest Hour

Aside from the birth of each of my three daughters, having my children see me graduate with my bachelor's degree was the highlight of my life. When I saw their faces just beaming with joy and pride that I had made such a major accomplishment in my life, I couldn't help but see the example I had become to the three of them. They were there with me from the beginning to the end. I have since gone on and graduated with my MBA and again, all three daughters were present. But nothing will ever surpass the joy and thrill of seeing them so excited over my bachelor's degree.

Another bright hour that continues to shine for me is to have the blessing of living near my three grandchildren. To be fortunate enough to watch my grandchildren grow from babies to teenagers and to have a relationship with them is a privilege that surpasses none other.

Lessons from the Light

I didn't feel like doing the official "walk" to receive my bachelors degree, but at the insistence of my children I did it anyway. As a result, I received more joy than I could ever imagine because of their delight at seeing their mother walk across the stage after so many years of hard work. So the lesson I learned was that sometimes if we do something for others – even when we don't feel like it – we may be the one who reaps the greatest benefit after all.

I also realized that even when we don't know it or pay attention, little eyes watch us. They watch what we say and do and it can either have a negative or a positive impact. It could even have a life-changing impact.

Biography

Marjorie Beckett was a single parent of three daughters, ages 3, 5 and 7 when her husband joined the ranks of "runaway dads." Previously a stay-at-home mom, she returned to the work force to support her family during one of the most trying times of her life.

Today, Marjorie is the assistant director for Alumni Affairs at Florida Institute of Technology. She has more than 24 years experience in higher education, including budget management, office management and personnel supervision. Marjorie is also the web master for the Alumni Affairs web site and has 16 years basic web page design, maintenance, and marketing and growth experience. She has also taught courses at both the university and at the local community college.

Marjorie has been on the board of directors for the Brevard Women's Center for the past five years and is active with her condo association. She also volunteers for the Florida Tech Women's Business Center and is a lifetime member of Delta Mu Delta. Marjorie is an advocate for the mentally ill as well as a supporter of the Arthritis Foundation.

She holds an A.S. and B.S. degree in business administration as well as an MBA with a minor in managing information technology.

Marjorie Beckett

Florida Institute of Technology
Office of Alumni Affairs
150 W University Blvd
Melbourne, FL, 32901
MarjorieBeckett@alumni.fit.edu

Chapter Seven

Catherine Behan, MS

Favorite Quote

"In this moment, I am safe, only good can come out of this situation and all is well. "—Louise Hay

When I stop and look at this very moment, and this moment alone, I know that it is true that I *am* safe and all *is* well, no matter what.

Passion

I am really lucky! I have been a change agent, a catalyst for countless creative people over the years. Whether teaching golf, counseling the parent of an autistic child, helping a woman find love for herself, assisting a professional adjust to being laid off and creating a new dream for the future, I have been privileged to be present for hundreds of "Aha" moments. I live for those moments. Being a part of connecting some critical inner dots for people seeking comfort during life transitions is my passion and I have been doing this work since I was knee-high.

Darkest Hour

At 55, I was a newlywed for the second time and living a dream life. My new husband and I had been married a year and a half and we had traveled near and far. From driving trips to San Francisco and Sedona to exotic jaunts to Hawaii and Saint Lucia, we were having the time of our lives. Both golfers, we felt we had been given the ultimate mulligan, a kind of life do-over, enabling us to build a relationship with the wisdom that comes with the gift of age.

I had been struggling with a very personal issue that I fondly nick-named "humorrhoids" for a long time, too long of a time, but the thought of treatment options kept me quiet and hurting. While in Saint Lucia, I promised my husband I would get them looked at and so I did. Bad news. Surgery, and yes it was every bit as bad as it could be.

That wasn't the worst of it though. After the surgery, the doctor had found something suspicious and ordered a biopsy. As I came to afterwards, my sweet husband, with tears in his eyes, said, "Cat? There's a problem...."

Really bad news. Rectal cancer. What? Are you kidding? Had the Universe played a final twisted trick that would tear us apart before we had a chance to begin? Why now? Why this?

Mercifully, in a strange sort of way the awful recovery from the surgery had me in such a fog, the full impact of the diagnosis didn't hit me for weeks. My husband, bless him, took me on as a project. He made spread sheets, for Pete's sake, keeping track of appointments, second opinions, CT scan reports. He drove me all over town seeking the best wisdom traditional medicine had to offer. Bless him, he kept bringing me flowers and cards even though I could barely appreciate them.

Seriously intimidated by the fact that what went in had to come out, I lost 10 pounds the hard way before treatment even began. I was weak and exhausted from the heavy pain medication I lived on. I had always been a confident, capable and resilient person, having proved it over and over. But now, sitting in the countless meetings with doctors talking about all that they had planned for me, I had panic attacks leaving me weeping in fear like a little child. I was reduced to embarrassingly public body problems; There is no dignity in rectal cancer treatment. Larry got to know me in more ways than I wanted him to.

Particularly troubling was the doc's description of the machinery that had been developed to make rectal replacement easier. As he showed me the diagrams of what would be left when he was done, I felt like he was talking about a car, not my body.

Chemo followed radiation before the surgeon took out my sick rectum and built a new one. Bowel retraining is something you never would imagine you would need. I went through months of humbling bathroom experiences, paper panties and all, leaving me with fading memories of sexy thongs and making love.

I don't think about that 18 months much. It seems like a thousand years ago. My treatments were successful and my body is operating beautifully. I am happy to say that Larry and I picked up our travel barely missing a beat when we spent our third anniversary in Italy, less than a year after my surgery.

In some ways, we are just starting to get back to us. Our relationship was deeply challenged and even went through a kind of dormancy. The image we had of each other changed as we took each step. But we are here, still standing and guess what? Romance is warming our hearts again, and with an even deeper appreciation we are planning our future.

Lessons from the Dark

I learned I am way stronger than I thought I was. For the first time in my life, I had a person who was there for me, even though I had nothing to bring to the table for months. I saw that I had spent all of my strength and energy acting like a kind and confident woman when the reality is, I *am* a kind and confident woman. I learned the difference between acting like a Soul Mate and being a Soul Mate. The lessons were tough, the tuition sky high, but being a graduate of the University of Cancer rocks!

Brightest Hour

It was a Christmas I will never forget.

My kids were 5 and 6 years old and I was in the midst of the super woman days. I made all my Christmas cards, decorated packages with glitter and bows, baked batches of Christmas cookies and volunteered to help with the school's Holiday Pageant.

Not being able to say no to anybody, I "volunteered" to collect donated food from the bowling league I belonged to and transport it to the area food bank. Having procrastinated a bit, it was now Monday of Christmas week and I was scrambling to find somewhere to donate the food.

Why, I don't know, but every food pantry I called was closed or not accepting donations. I was exhausted and frustrated. Plus I was angry at myself for waiting until the last minute and felt responsible to the group to get this food to needy people before Christmas.

After 10 phone calls, I finally was connected to a Hmong family living in a distressed area of town. Frazzled and struggling, yet still clinging to the desire to teach my kids the true meaning of Christmas, I asked them to look in their rooms for a couple of books or outgrown toys to bring to this family of 12.

My kids brought me a handful of broken crayons.

Are you kidding?

Fiercely protective of their belongings, they were unable to understand the request. "But these are *my* toys; I don't want to give them away."

Becoming more frustrated by the moment, I was becoming harsh with the kids and then of course was feeling guilty for being such a grouch. *Merry Christmas.*

Steaming, I piled all of us into the car, loaded all the food and off we went. It was raining and we were stopped in traffic. My daughter asked where we were going and I explained about the part of the city the family lived in and why things were tough for them. In the midst of my explanation, I mentioned that they lived on 34th street.

"Mommy!" she gasped with wonder, "Our own *Miracle on 34th Street.*"

My mood instantly melted as my heart registered what she said. Hot tears filled my eyes. We were making a miracle – procrastination, broken crayons and all. The real meaning of Christmas *was* there....in spite of all my plans and excuses.

As we carried bag after bag of groceries into the house, the gratitude on the face of the pregnant mother of the brood was unmistakable. Understanding not a word of English, she kept thanking us over and over in her native language. The look in her eyes was enough. We knew we were in exactly the right place.

When I tucked the kids into bed that night, I hugged them extra hard.

How did I get so wrapped up in my inconvenience and create such a drama out of the whole thing? Thank goodness for a miracle on 34th street.

Lessons from the Light

This lesson, like all of my lessons from the light, is about LIGHTENING UP. Over and over, I get wrapped up in drama. Simple circumstances get spun like cotton candy into sticky icky messes. I was the one who procrastinated. I didn't plan in advance. I didn't take the time to work with the kids to pick toys they could part with.

If I could talk to me back then I would say, "Everything is going to be OK, no matter what. Try not to worry and obsess over things. Things always work out." You know why? Because they do.

Biography

Catherine writes, "I never dreamed I would be divorced at 50. I also did not expect to move across the country, land in San Diego and fall in love again. Imagine my surprise when I realized that one of my golfing buddies was interested in me! As I slowly learned to reopen my heart and let love in again, I responded to this gentle man's love and allowed myself to trust once more. Could I have met ANOTHER soul mate?"

Now remarried, Catherine is learning to be a true soul mate and finds that intention brings out the best in her man and in her relationship. She is an e-columnist, inspirational speaker and relationship coach.

Catherine Behan, MS

The Savvy Soul Mate
858-405-3723
Catherine@soulmatesavvy.com
www.savvysoulmate.com

Chapter Eight

Salee Brenner

Favorite Quote

Two favorite quotes that have supported my journey are: "God is Love." the Holy Bible – and "All you need is love." the Beatles. It sounds too simple to be true. And what is love anyway? However, in some of my deepest moments of despair, these words inspired me.

Passion

My life's passion has always been people. I have been intrigued by the diversity of people and celebrate the unlimited possibilities of each one. I am truly fascinated with the stellar variety of colors, costumes, customs, cuisines, ceremonies, and communities that exist. I rejoice in the uniqueness of each individual and revere the oneness of us all. I believe that we are undeniably connected by the thread of Divine love. It is my heart's desire to heal and to help others, encouraging their vibrant wisdom to surface with grace and honor. I know that each and every one is precious, making a difference in this world, one choice at a time. Allow me to support you to celebrate your choices; they are magnificent as are you!

Darkest Hour

At age 20, and for the following 11 years, I lived with a man who was mentally, emotionally and physically abusive. My frustrations developed into fits of rage which resulted in me spewing insults on my loved ones. We had six children together and lived like nomads, really more like vagrants. A nine-foot by 12-foot tent was our home for months at a time, we lived off of other people's charity and welfare was our main source of financial income. It was an incredibly stressful lifestyle dominated with chaos, addictions, and abuse. I acknowledge that my consciousness was not very developed and that most of my choices were made out of fear. I have come to a place of honor and self-acceptance, taking full responsibility for who I was and how I behaved.

Finally, I gained the courage to leave my husband after dozens of previous attempts. I secured a small modest cabin in the mountains for me and my children. My oldest daughter, who was 10 at the time, wanted to stay with her dad, and so she did. In less than a year I received an alarming phone call informing me that my daughter and husband were being held in custody. He was charged and later convicted of sexually abusing her. YES! This was one of my darkest hours. The previous 11 years of abuse paled in comparison to this grievous assault. The suffering this experience brought on my family is difficult to describe. The guilt and shame that I carried for years did not quickly disappear. And, my beloved daughter is still imprisoned with a life of mental anguish. There is so much suffering and pain in the world and it does not serve us to try to deny it. I believe that it is valuable to be able to feel it, embrace it with compassion, and move on. I had repeated opportunity to release my judgments of right or wrong and allow love to heal my heart wounds.

What a nightmare I had created. I was in my early thirties, a single mother of six, and feeling totally incapable of moving forward. I believed I needed help raising my children and so I married again. The truth is that this man had similar values and beliefs as my first husband, and was equally assaulting. Very clearly I had not taken the time to go inside myself to discover the parts of me that needed healing. I had not taken the time to unveil the parts of myself that attracted yet another dysfunctional relationship. I had not taken the time to discover the truth of my being and the depth of my passion. Thirteen years of battling with fears and depression passed before realizing that I could make a different choice.

Lessons from the Dark

I had to surrender any false notions of blame and victimization before I could make the conscious choice to divorce myself from yet another relationship based on lies. I spent a lot of energy running from my feelings rather than honoring them. This is unproductive, as our emotions are loaded with information that can serve us on our journey to enlightenment. I still continue to meditate on this quote, *Esprit Devaji*, "Anything but unconditional love is abuse." The implications of this belief touch deeply into the core of my being.

Brightest Hour

Another quote, from Rev. Terry Cole Whitaker, whose essence and truth has given me courage, is, "What you think of me is none of my business." I have spent much of my life looking for validation outside of myself, from parents, friends, teachers and society in general. I would compare myself to others, striving to measure up, somehow always seeming to fall short. This pattern only created more strife, limitations and bitterness within. It is really not important at all what others think of you. It is simply their opinion which is based on their values and judgments.

Fact is, the person most affected by judgments is the one holding them. It is not the truth of who you are. What is important is how you perceive yourself. Again, for many moons I believed myself to be stupid, unworthy, and unlovable. I have come to know that each one of us has the ability to be accountable for how we respond to life. Our consciousness is the creative force that manifests our current experiences. So revel in the awesomeness of your creation!

Although my life was at times tumultuous, those chaotic experiences paved the way to my "Brightest Hour," which was when I realized that I had the freedom to create whatever experiences I desire. I don't recall the exact moment, but at some point my consciousness shifted and I was aware that the common thread in these 24 years of marriage was me. That truly there is no thing outside of me, and I am the center of my own universe. Yes, I really started to get the picture that I was the one in charge of my life. I also know, with that awareness comes the privilege of taking responsibility for my invention. Personal expansion is an ongoing process, one choice at a time. I'm not sure if I will ever be completely "there," wherever "there" is. Actually, I'm convinced that the "there" is the *now*. Thankfully, I am no longer subject to fits of rage and my adult children are making responsible choices for their lives. I am a work in progress, changing from breath to breath. It is liberating to get to be me and give others the same respect. Every day there is opportunity to open my heart, to enlarge my vision, and to serve those around me. I hold my past with the highest reverence, as a beloved teacher and friend. I also welcome all the wondrous experiences that are yet to be created. I find that tears, gratitude, and laughter make my life a more joyful expression.

Lessons from the Light

At age 60 I am experiencing more insight, confidence, and peace than ever before. I'm able to see that all of my choices have been based on my perceptions. And as my perceptions have changed over the years, so have my experiences. My journey has been filled with many "Dark Hours" and just as many "Bright Hours." I believe that these moments are all equally precious and valuable to my personal expansion. As a matter of fact, at this stage of life I no longer hold any judgment on them as good or bad. They just are. All of my choices have served me. Of course, some of them brought more joy into my life and others were more painful. But they have been the steps that I created for myself one decision at a time, that have brought me to the now.

Biography

Salee has practiced holistic health care for the past 20 years. She gives nurturing massage therapy, shares nutritional insight, imparts information on relaxation techniques and lifestyle choices, and encourages balanced wellness. As Salee teaches others she continues to learn. She loves being of service to family and clients. Her creativity is expressed through photography, crafting, rock carving, drumming, and dancing. She has been blessed with eight incredible grandchildren who help her to connect with the simple pleasures in life and unconditional love.

Salee Brenner

saleemimi@yahoo.com
(321) 693-8199

Chapter Nine

Claire Ellis

Favorite Quote

"Use what talents you possess; the woods would be very silent if no birds sang except those that sang best."—Henry Van Dyke

Passion

My life has always been about service to others. As a child, helping others was instilled in me by my mother, who was a wonderful role model. As a former exceptional education teacher, I felt called to help and understand children who fell out of the norm. My desire to help others also extended to being a Hospice volunteer and companion to the elderly. Today I am helping improve the status of women through my affiliation with Zonta International.

Darkest Hour

The lowest point in my life dragged across a 30-day period between the ends of January and February 2003, when my husband John and I lost four loved ones, including both our moms who died four days apart. We spent 30 days crisscrossing the country trying to be in all places at once. It all began when a longtime friend died suddenly in Connecticut while I was visiting my sister and Mom in Chicago. Tony's death was a shock. He was my contemporary and I wasn't ready to think about my generation beginning to depart this life.

Mom was living with my sister and was in the late stages of Alzheimer's disease. I had been visiting for two weeks and I knew Mom's time was short. When I left for Tony's funeral, I planned to return to Chicago. God had other plans. While in Connecticut, my husband John called to tell me that his mom was critical and we had to leave for Texas. I returned to Florida and we were on the road west the next day. I called Irene to check on my mother and to tell her I would return to Chicago as soon as I could. When we got to Texas, we knew John's mom's time was very short. But I thought I could still make it back to Chicago before my mother died. I made reservations to travel on Valentine's Day, our 15th wedding anniversary. John would stay in Texas and we would just go day-by-day.

I didn't make it in time. My mother died at 1 a.m. February 14. I went in to tell Mom Ellis I was leaving and she said, "Don't worry, God won't take us both on the same day." John and I were so distraught and didn't know how we would get through the next few days without each other. My grief was overwhelming as I was not there when the angels came for my Mom. And how could it happen on Valentine's Day? It had been one of the happiest days of my life. As I returned with my family from Mom's wake four days later, John called to tell me Mom Ellis had also died. She would be flown to Milwaukee to be laid next to Dad. There would be no time to spend with my sister after Mom's funeral.

John flew to Chicago and together we drove to Milwaukee. As we were pulling into a motel, my cell phone rang. It was John's son telling us that John's mentor in Judo and long time friend Tai was gravely ill and wasn't expected to make it through the night. We checked in in silence and were feeling so forlorn. We just lay there staring at the ceiling unable to sleep. I found a Bible there and opened it to Psalms and started reading them aloud. If there was one either of us found comforting I would read it again. This is how we got through the night. We were unable to make it back to Florida for Tai's funeral.

Lessons from the Dark

I finally have come to understand that Mom's death on Valentine's Day was a gift of love and a way we would stay forever connected. I know now that both our moms would want John and me to go on and celebrate life and our love together. My sister Irene and I are much closer now, and Tony's wife Pat and I have a renewed friendship. At the moment of darkness, no good can be seen, but it will come in time. It is the cycle of life.

Brightest Hour

Back in the mid '80s, I joined a motivational marketing company called Gathering of Eagles. That proved to be a life-changing experience. The company offered a series of self-improvement courses including: self-awareness, self-discovery, self-development, leadership and health. Once purchased, you could participate in any of the classes whenever they were offered, with no limitations.

During my first "adventure" as they were called, the instructor told us, "You are where you are because you choose to be." I took issue with that statement and could not understand the concept. I knew I was unhappy, but I sure knew who was to blame and it wasn't me. I kept attending the adventures over and over and one day I had the proverbial "AHA!" moment. I understood that I *was* responsible for the direction of my life. My transformation was apparent and I was selected to attend a leadership training course.

The leadership training classes were structured to overcome fear and build confidence. This particular class was held in California and the adventure was built around learning to hang glide. Even though no pressure was brought to bear, all 20 who attended the class decided to try it. We were first shown a video on the basics of hang gliding. The next lesson was assembling your own hang glider. That really frightened me, because I had no confidence that I could put it together properly. The instructors did thoroughly check our work to make sure we were all flight worthy.

My basic flight instructions were given to me while I was being harnessed into my glider. "Do not hold the bar tightly, but very lightly," I was told. "You can then gently steer and control the glider. If you hold the bar tightly you will cause the glider to crash, as a tight grip will pull the glider over your body." I could not fathom not holding on for dear life. As a result, I crashed in a cow field and slid into the cow pies. The instructor found me and told me to drag my glider back up the hill and try it again. When ready again, he reminded me of the instructions and asked if I now believed I could do it. I said I would still hang on tight. I crashed again and now was even more covered in cow manure. As I pulled my glider back up the hill, everyone was avoiding me – I smelled so bad. The instructor asked me again if I believed. Finally, I said, "Yes I believe!" and barely touched the bar. What happened then was amazing. I began soaring and screaming at the same time. It's called, "whiting out." I was able to land my glider safely without landing in the cow pies or falling over. I was a graduate!

Lessons from the Light

The lesson could not have been clearer to me. Level of Belief = Level of Success.

Biography

Claire earned a B.S. in Education and M.S. in Exceptional Education from Indiana University and taught for 15 years. Since leaving the classroom, she has held positions in sales and marketing and instructed self-improvement classes. Today, she owns a home-based Shaklee business and is co-owner of Turtle Mound Flutes with her husband John, who has a grown son and daughter. Her daughter Andrea is a senior attending Rollins College.

Claire was inspired by Kelly Palace and the women she met at an e-Women Network event to start reaching for her dream of being a writer. This is her first published work.

Claire is a member of several civic and networking groups and has volunteered for Hospice. She is president of the Zonta Club of Melbourne, Fla. She attends St. Katherine Greek Orthodox Church and is a member of St. Sophia Philoptochos and the Greek American Association of Brevard.

Claire Ellis

cellis1988@earthlink.net
321-254-0284
shaklee.net/retisoft

Chapter Ten

Grace Marie Graziano

Favorite Quote

"Great women are not considered so because of personal achievements but for the effect their efforts have had on the lives of countless others. From daring feats of bravery to the understated ways of a compassionate heart, great women possess a common strength of character. Through their passion and persistence, they have advanced womanhood and the world."— *Peggy Anderson.*

Passion

This particular quote means a lot to me because I have seen firsthand that women, including myself, can make a difference. Don't under estimate your potential. Just look within and see how marvelous you are. The passion of encouraging another is my life's work. The legacy we leave as women will long be remembered by our children's children and beyond. By encouraging one another, we can then inspire, motivate, and build each other up for peace and harmony in our lives. I encourage you to be alert to life, enjoy nature, and realize the gifts that have been given to us by our Creator.

Darkest Hour

In 1976, our family moved from New York to Satellite Beach, Fla., a beautiful bedroom community conducive to raising children – five to be exact. We were the typical middle class, roof over our heads, food on the table, dog, cat, gerbils, trying to make ends meet, kind of a family. We did all the right things, including going to church on a regular basis. However, by 1981, it was obvious that my marriage was on shaky ground. The first in what was to become a trilogy of pain came in June 1982: a broken marriage after 25 years. I decided to launch myself into the real estate business, opening a Century 21 office, which was very popular at the time and very expensive. I was busy setting up an office, hiring staff and beginning to generate income.

My children introduced me to their friend's father, and in all my vulnerability, I fell madly in love in the spring of 1983, the second in the trilogy. Planning a New Year's Eve wedding at the end of that year, it was excitement and heaven on Earth. A week before the wedding, family issues arose and it was clear we needed to postpone. Invitations, dress, catering, all up in smoke. Months went by and we thought how romantic a beach wedding sounded, so we set a date in July. Well, that did not work out either. Labor Day was approaching and Century 21 was offering a special training in Atlanta the day after Labor Day for the remaining week. We elected to marry in Atlanta and then stay for the training and honeymoon at the same time.

It was a hot summer day a few days before Labor Day and I was putting up shelves in the back room when a strange woman came into the office. Asking if I could help her, she proceeded to give me explicit details of her relationship with my beloved, the man I was going to marry in a few days. She went on for what seemed like an eternity. I finally "came to" and asked her to leave. Confronting Mr. Beloved, his response was that he loved both of us and could not live without either one of us. I said he could have her 100 percent.

I drove to my friend's home and collapsed in her waiting arms. Unable to function, I was hospitalized with extreme trauma affecting my speech and motor skills. I was released on bed rest until I was strong enough to walk.

The third in the trilogy came on Saturday, the week after Labor Day, September 1984. My son was out with friends, my one twin daughter was out and my younger twin daughter was milling around the house. It was about 2 in the afternoon and I was in bed reliving the nightmare events of the last 12 days. My nightstand was filled with bottles of medication. One to help me sleep, one to keep me functioning, and one to calm me down. I looked at these bottles for what seemed a very long time. I took the help-me-sleep bottle in my hand, looked at it and clasped it tightly next to my body. I just didn't have the will to go on. My heart was broken so severely it astounded me.

Lessons from the Dark

I knew my daughter would be leaving soon for cheerleading practice and then I could be alone. This would be easy, just take some pills and fall asleep. I was ready; I couldn't understand what was taking her so long to leave the house. I had a glass of water on the table and my focus was on it and the bottle I was holding in my hand. My daughter finally came in to say goodbye. She hugged me and said she was off to cheerleading.

It was then that my lesson from the dark gave way to my brightest hour. As my daughter approached the door, she abruptly turned around, looked right at me and said, "I love you, Mom." I said almost automatically, "I love you, too." I heard the door close and uncapped the bottle, closing my eyes for a moment when suddenly my daughter's face was crystal clear standing at the doorway saying, "I love you," again and again and again. While I was fixed on seeing her face, God's voice called audibly and absolute, *Please do not do this. Please do not do this to yourself and your child. She will not survive it and two lives will be lost.* The bottle dropped from my hand onto the floor and I began sobbing for help, *Father, I need Your help. Please give me the strength and opportunity to get through this.*

Brightest Hour

With all the love and comfort God provides, I knew He would be there for me if I just let Him into my heart. He and I talked for a long time. I thought for sure He would be angry with me for forgetting Him so many times these last few years. With the intervention of God understanding the pain of my trauma and the impending pain of my child, I believe God saved me that day using my child's face and words to bring me back to life.

It was hours before anyone returned home and as they came in, one by one, I embraced them and told them that I loved them so much and that we were going to start anew.

Losing thousands of dollars, I could not save my business. My son and I tried to resurrect the pieces but it went down the tubes. I closed the office and planned to make a new start in Orlando. Yes, my life began anew that day with the help of therapy and the devotion of our Father; I was able to get through this difficult time. He instilled very deeply in my heart and soul that He is always there for us, we just need to ask for His help. He is there to wipe away the tears, mend the broken heart, and give us the strength to go on when we do not think there is another ounce of strength left in our bones.

Moving to Orlando was the best thing in the world, starting with a wonderful marketing job, turning it into an esteemed career, gaining recognition beyond my expectation, and finding a new path leading me to teaching the different personality types, speaking, coaching, writing with four published works. I now share encouraging words to my audience instilling "Yes, you can."

Lessons from the Light

In this journey of life, I have learned that it is a wasted day when you cannot laugh, learn something new, and find something or someone to love. What I also know for sure is that we always have choices and keeping faith, joy and love in the forefront of our life is essential to our well-being. There is a verse in the Bible that says "Let no corrupt words come out of your mouths, only words to edify and lift up". That is my motto, my passion and words that I try to live by everyday. I believe that the experiences we have are for our greater purpose in life. To further our growth as a spiritual being living a human life. To finally know and accept that God is with us always in dark and light times, developing our endurance in this life of ours. How can I serve? That is a question God loves to hear.

Biography

Grace Marie Graziano is a speaker, author and certified personality trainer. She is listed in the 1998 *Who's Who International* and has received many awards for outstanding and committed service. Grace's new endeavor is "Coaching with Grace." She partners with clients to help them discover and enhance their potential to become all that they were meant to be. She is a contributing author of *"Getting Along with Almost Anybody,"* and *"God Allows U-Turns-American Moments,"* as well as author of *"TGIF-Love Notes to my Friends and Family* and *"TGIF - 101 Inspirational Thoughts With Love."*

Grace Marie Graziano

www.gracegraziano.com
gmgraz1@bellsouth.net

Chapter Eleven

Dr. Beckie M. Grgich

Favorite Quote

"The world breaks everyone and afterward many are strong in the broken places."—Ernest Hemingway

Passion

I am passionate as I strive to support and challenge others. I believe if you meet people where they are in their lives, the learning will be maximized.

If people are working diligently themselves, they are worth supporting. I will lend a hand, offer assistance and perhaps even do things on their behalf.

If people are looking for assistance with no personal effort, they must instead be challenged. I encourage them to find strength, find ways to learn and grow. I entice a spirit of cooperation and movement toward personal goals.

Darkest Hour

It was a springtime afternoon and I was 15 years old. My biggest worries were my social life and summer plans. My dad had to work three hours away to support the family due to drastic layoffs in Salt Lake City.

The phone rang and my mother answered. All I heard her say was, "Oh no, no, no." Tears were streaming down her face as she told me my brother had choked on a sandwich at school. He was dead. I held my body stiff and maintained strong emotional composure. I had to find a way to help my parents and sister through this. I planned to deal with myself later.

We made it through planning the funeral, attending the services and attempting to resume life. But life as we knew it completely changed. My father fell apart through his depression. He started drinking. He stopped coming home on weekends. He sent a messenger and I answered the door and was served my mom's divorce papers. The money stopped coming and we started selling our belongings to pay the bills.

One dark evening, I found myself listening to my mother tell me that I would probably be better off with my father because she didn't have the means to support me. I remember feeling all alone and abandoned. My mother withdrew from me emotionally. She wanted the pain to be over and I feared she wanted to die. I knew we were in trouble. My mother had been stretched to her utter limits.

As days stretched into months I watched my mother dig deep within herself to find strength that even she did not know existed. She hired the toughest attorney in town, made some financial changes and pushed forward. I was proud to see the strength in her. My father later told me, as he sat alone without his family he was overcome with harsh feelings of fear and evil. He said the experience was so dark and intense, he knew he had to make severe changes. My father stopped drinking, fired his attorney and moved toward reconciliation with my mother. My mother somehow found it in herself to work toward mending her relationship with him. They worked diligently together. I respected them for giving me time to heal and gradually work toward reunification with both of them about a year later.

My world became something I never imagined. My sense of stability was forever changed. Despite my injuries, I also learned a great lesson about a person's ability to heal. I found that my love for our united family was more important than all the mistakes each person made alone. I discovered great respect and dedication for the both of them, individually and united.

Lessons from the Dark

I discovered ways to cherish the smallest of moments with loved ones. I chose to never be financially dependent upon another person. I pursued an education and attained a career of motivation and understanding.

I was given the gift of forgiveness. I also realized that failing to see the good that comes with strife would limit my growth. My parents were in love. They failed to come together during their loss, but they learned. They continue to live as husband and wife and have in recent years experienced some of the greatest joys of their 45 years together and counting.

Brightest Hour

While at breakfast with a friend in 2002 I found myself tearfully discussing my wonder and concern as to whether or not I would ever be able to have a child. I was in my 30's, had been with my partner for years and had undergone countless tests and procedures to ensure that childbearing was possible. After years of helping others with their children's problems as a child psychologist, I prayed for the chance to be able to be a mother to my own child. I also knew there was the potential that I would need to redesign my own plans, moving forward as a couple with no children of our own. I began considering other life options and possibilities such as taking more couples vacations, volunteering for youth organizations, taking jobs around the world and more.

In late 2003 I took a pregnancy test and could not believe the results! I then took three more tests and the results were all the same, positive for pregnancy. I excitedly made an appointment with my physician and waited another six weeks for the results confirmed. The news was positive.

I spent the duration of the pregnancy glowing with great joy and excitement. When others attempted to tell me their personal, miserable pregnancy stories, I smiled. None of that mattered. I was going to be a mother. I didn't mind the changes in my body. I excitedly read books about the months to come. I celebrated each milestone. At last, on September 15, 2004, I held him in my arms, a sweet little boy full of life.

I found strength in knowing that no matter what happens in this life, there is a way to redefine my path and the paths of others. Perhaps I am faced with challenges so that I actually end up where I am supposed to be, instead of where I wanted to be. Perhaps I needed to learn the intensity of the pain involved with being childless so that I could teach another person how to work through this difficulty.

Lessons from the Light

I learned that it's OK to maintain hope for the possibilities in life. I found one of the greatest joys, motherhood, by holding on to the possibility that it could happen. I also found that with motherhood also comes a deep and intense sense of mortality. I have never worried so much, loved so much or cared so much about any one thing, and the feelings intensified with our second child, a baby girl.

Biography

Dr. Beckie M. Grgich, Psy.D. is a Psychologist and Life Coach working with children, teens, adults and seniors. Dr. Grgich enjoys a challenge. She has the ability to find a silver lining in the most difficult of circumstances. She finds strength and power from within individuals and works to magnify their abilities and sense of wellbeing.

Dr. Beckie M. Grgich

P.O. Box 939
Pahrump, NV 89041
775-751-1349

Chapter Twelve

Rev. Elizabeth Hess Stamper, MS, LCSW

Favorite Quote

Even if you were cooking dinner for yourself, alone in your house, why move as less than love's open dance while offering your heart's yearning brighter than the sun shines? You can open as pleasure, move as a goddess, wash soapsuds off your dishes as if making exquisite love – you can live open as love's art, moving in every aspect of life as a reflection of the sacred. ~ David Deida

Passion

I believe in the essential goodness of people, and that our true nature is blissful, peaceful, loving and wise. We are each divinely created and infinitely creative. All our problems stem from the moments we forgot this truth and believed instead in separateness, littleness and lack. My passion is creating the safe, sacred space in which the individual can release the layers "forgetting," or repressed emotions, the wounds of this world, and the false beliefs, and touch once again the beauty and freedom of the inner Self. My joy is facilitating events where people can share their beauty and their gifts in community, uplifting each other and changing the world.

Darkest Hour

It is an endless September night and I am lying on a single bed in the back room of my uncle's small house. My daughter sleeps in the bed next to me so, even though I can't stop shivering, I don't make a sound. I'm not cold – it is Florida, after all – *I am just so afraid.* Afraid in a way that I've never felt before. The kind of fear that always arises – to some degree or another – whenever our world turns upside down and the self we thought we knew (and were) is no longer the self who stares back at us from the mirror.

About month before I had come here with my three kids because I had nowhere else to go – my uncle was staying up north for a while so we had this place to live. *For now.* Then who knows? Maybe my husband and I would reconcile and he would be willing, as he said, "to let me back in the state." It seemed the only solution that would make my children happy and help them forgive me for ruining their lives. Even though he and I were so estranged from each other that the thought of a reunion made it hard to breathe – what else could I do? How would I live? *Who would I be?*

My "identity" for the first 15 years of my marriage had been loyal wife, loving mother, and devoted follower of my spiritual teacher (not necessarily in that order). But lying there, night after night, on that small bed, I could no longer see myself as loyal, loving and "spiritual" when I had so deeply hurt those whom I loved the most. I hadn't meant to, of course. Who ever does? My crime had been to let unspoken and unresolved grievances pile up between my husband and me. It had seemed far easier to ignore problems and repress difficult feelings than to summon the courage to confront, communicate, own my own projections and truly, deeply forgive. When we have an unhealed wound "caused" by someone in the past – who may not even have intended it – we can project that pain into a current experience – with someone who again may not have intended it, and we are doomed to relive this pain until we can become aware and be set free. And so, we had let the spirit of real intimacy between us die from neglect, cowardice and our complementary forms of emotional immaturity. *Until* a huge wake-up call came in the form of my attraction to another man. Even though I didn't act on that attraction, I had to be honest about it, and the emotional betrayal my husband felt was devastating.

So, had our marriage died? Had my treacherous heart dealt the final blow? Or was it just in a coma and could be resuscitated, with enough work, commitment, patience, atonement and love? My children adored their father, who adored them and was now a thousand miles away. How could I have let this happen? Night after night, as my mind raced and my body shivered, I held on as best I could, using every prayer and spiritual practice I knew until morning came. Miraculously, it always did. And slowly, through prayer and practice, a faith emerged that allowed a new life and a more authentic *me* to unfold.

Lessons from the Dark

Who would I be? The pivotal times in life always involve an identity crisis, the unmasking and eventual letting go of a "false self" that is based on who we think we *should* be in order to get the love, approval, and security that we need to survive. In my dark nights, as I learned to *breathe through* fear and self-doubt, I opened to the first glimmerings of a self-acceptance not based on *shoulds*. Under the layers of conditioned mind, I found an innately peaceful and trusting consciousness. Finding this Self within me was also the doorway to finding and trusting it in others, thus allowing for the possibility of relationships based on openness, transparency and real love. Spirit teaches that "what is Real can't be threatened" and finding that Real is both the challenge and the *invitation* of every dark night.

Brightest Hour

One morning, after wrestling with the deep grief and pain of an "ending," I lay on my bed exhausted. I realized that the thing I wanted most in the whole world would not happen – at least not in the way I *thought* it should – and somehow (perhaps only by the grace of utter fatigue), I surrendered to that fact. All of a sudden, I became aware of a light in the room. My eyes were closed and at first I thought that the sun had come from behind some clouds and was brightening the room. But it got even brighter—it was a beautiful golden light—and with it came a feeling of peace. I realized it was not a physical light because my eyes were still closed as it continued to brighten and envelop me until I felt myself let go and relax into its gentle, radiant embrace. *If God were holding you,* I thought, *it would feel just like this.*

I lay there for a long time. At one point, a bird started to sing outside the window. As I was listening to it, I realized I was also *feeling* the birdsong and the sound caused wave after wave of pleasure to flow through my body. The bird flew away, and then a moment later, I heard a truck rumbling along on a nearby highway. Incredibly, the sound of the truck engendered the same feeling of visceral joy as the birdsong! Every breath seemed to take me deeper into a state of quiet bliss. After a while, the pull of "my day" got bigger than my awareness of the energy, so I got up and went downstairs to start some paperwork. I turned the CD player on, but as soon as the music started, the vibrations started again, too. So, I lay down in the middle of the kitchen floor and surrendered (once again) to the waves of sound, light and bliss moving through my body.

Eventually, I started to come back to "normal consciousness" but the awe of that experience has never left me. To remember how light and peace and joy came to me in such a powerful, *sensual* and unexplainable way, is to feel immense love for life, and humble and grateful to God. It is to know that the Sacred lives within me as surely as I live within It and *that I do not have to leave my body to feel Its Presence.* In fact, perhaps the deepest and most mysterious aspect of life in this form, is that it is perfectly engineered for the most delicious experiencing of God. Why else would we choose to come here and be embodied? If not to know God with *all* that we are – mind and body, heart and soul – and, through that knowing, to feel how completely and unconditionally *loved* we are.

Lessons from the Light

We have all heard, "Ask and it shall be given." But when we don't receive, we assume our asking was not heard and nothing was given. But the truth is that when we don't receive, it's because we are holding onto an energy that disallows our receiving. Because of the universal Law of Attraction, *like attracts like*, so the energy of "not having" can only be met with more "not having."

I had been asking for love. As long as I held onto the painful feeling of "unloved," there was no space within me to receive. But when I let go – *thank you, Oh Spirit of Exhaustion!* – Love flooded into me. Love as light, as comfort, as pleasure, as peace. And finally, with my complete surrender, love came in and through me as pure joy.

With lots of practice, it has become easier to let go of what I don't want (although sometimes I still need the aid of a sleepless night), and to turn my attention toward what makes me feel good. The more I do this, the more experiences I have of receiving what I want, and the easier it is to find good-feeling things to focus on. But the most powerful insight gained from this experience is that the Universal Law is set up not to punish us, but to help us achieve our heart's desire. As we learn to trust this, moments of disappointment, frustration or emptiness more easily give way to acceptance of what is, to turning toward what could be, and finally, to allowing in the next expression *and* fulfillment of our ever-expanding appetite for joy.

Biography

Rev. Elizabeth Hess Stamper, MS, LMHC, maintains a private practice in psychotherapy in Florida, specializing in women's issues, relationships, intentional living and spiritual awakening. She has a Master's degree in counseling, and has been a student of meditation and yoga since 1972. Elizabeth has been exploring the powerful healing potential and sacred dimension of the breath for over 20 years, and of energy healing for the last 10. She has authored a well-received book on spiritual relationships and two meditation CDs, and has been leading workshops and retreats for 15 years. For her work in helping to create and promote community, Elizabeth was recently given the "Heart of the Community" award by the Brevard Chapter of Conscious Living Partnership.

Rev. Elizabeth Hess Samper, MS, LCSW
eliz121@juno.com
www.ahealingcircle.com
321.777.6216.

Chapter Thirteen

Esther Levy

Favorite Quote

"Be the change that you want to see in the world."—Mohandas Gandhi

Passion

My life passion is personal growth and development and seeking truth through the study of the Kabbalah and other spiritual teachings. My solution is living in a life of abundance and prosperity, using tools like honesty and integrity in a world that is full of only illusion and fear.

Darkest Hour

I lived at home with my mom, dad and sister and the dog always at my beck and call. I had everything, but I still hungered to grow up and leave home to get away from the control of two very loving parents. I met a very nice young man who after a very short time became my husband. We thought we loved each other for the right reasons, but time showed us differently. We fought most of the time. Money was limited and I became sick with a condition that even the doctors didn't understand. The condition was called immune thrombocytopenic purpura (ITP), an autoimmune disorder characterized by low platelet counts.

I had always been a healthy, active person, so for me this was a huge shock. My relationship seemed to get a little better at this point because no one wanted to upset me. My husband was now very kind, loving and patient. As I began to take the horrible treatments which included Prednisone, a common treatment used for this condition, I retained water and was swollen most of the time. I looked as if I had gained 50 pounds. The hair on my body became very dark and thick and I started to develop male characteristics. I was super insecure and constantly looked for love and approval from my husband to make me feel beautiful and good enough while I was going through this crazy process.

I was treated differently due to the excess weight and due to the illness. Finally after many months, I did get better. We moved from my idyllic hometown in Maryland to Miami because my husband wanted to be close to his family. I now had to leave the security of my home and I was very sad. When we arrived at the home of my mother-in-law I was devastated. It looked like a war camp.

There were high fences everywhere and I thought that my life was over. I was in a depressed state for many weeks. Finally, I got back to work and things seemed to get back to normal, until I started to realize my marriage was not OK. I began to imagine myself leaving him and soon enough I found myself wanting to be with other men.

It was never about sex or just the physical desire. It was that I wasn't getting the love or the complete union and partnership that a man and a woman must have when they are married.

We started going to a therapist to help the marriage and we discovered the Kabbalah. It was the most important thing that could have ever happened to me. But for him it was hell. I began to grow spiritually and we began to grow apart. He was not ready to move to the next level and so our marriage ended after seven years. It was a very painful process and I felt like a failure. However, it was exactly the lesson I needed to get to *my* next level.

Lessons from the Dark

The main lesson I learned from my darkest hour was that I can control my own faith and destiny with the help of the Universe. I was the one who could change the movie of my life in a blink of an eye. When I was sick I waited for the doctors to fix me. In my marriage I blamed my husband for not working hard enough or being good enough. And I expected him to make me feel beautiful. I waited for everyone else to take care of me.

I was always unhappy and never stopped to ask myself why this was happening to me and whether I had a part in it. I considered myself a huge victim. However, I have no regrets. I am stronger and wiser now, and able to help so many others by what I went through. Also, I now appreciate my ex-husband and everyone else for being part of my process.

Brightest Hour

I went to a friend's birthday party and was introduced to a young man whom I felt I knew from before, but I knew that couldn't be. He was in a relationship so we kept our distance.

Suddenly out of the blue, a few couples that were part of my circle of friends began to break up. My future-husband was one of those couples, and surprisingly my two -year relationship ended as well two weeks later.

We now were both single and started hanging out at parties, having a short conversation here and there. One day we ended up going to the beach together and had our first date that night. We went to my parents' home where I was living at the time and had dinner, and it felt like it was always supposed to be this way. Both of us felt something unexplainable but so right.

As time went on, we spent a lot of time talking, thinking and analyzing about whether this relationship should move forward. No matter how hard times were we never once said we wanted anyone else. One year later we were more in love than ever and decided to get married.

Money was tight. We had two months to create the most memorable event of our lives. Everything was perfect except that he never proposed. I had always wanted the formal proposal I never had in my previous relationship. I wanted it to be perfect – the proposal, the ring the whole deal. But given the money situation I knew it would have to be a total miracle to get a ring.

A few months prior, he had given me a ring and earrings for my birthday. I thought I could give him back that ring and let him propose with it. As the wedding date got closer I became more anxious about him proposing. I would hint to him almost every day. He finally got upset and told me he didn't want to talk about it anymore. I swore to myself that I would let go and let G-d.

I then decided he was more important to me than any ring or proposal. I knew he loved me with all his heart and if he could he would give me everything. The next day was Thanksgiving and we were planning to go to an important meeting about the traditional Kabbalistic wedding and have dinner at my parents' house. We spoke a lot that day about the progress of the wedding and our own personal preparation as we got closer to our big day.

I felt we really reconnected on that day. It was now around 6 p.m. and we were on our way to the meeting. It was a very powerful night because it was the beginning of the new month of Sagittarius, which is the month of miracles. Also, it was the month of our wedding, and there happened to be a wedding going on in the same place as the meeting. Let's just say all the stars were aligned. As we finished the meeting, we got to the car to head over to my parents home for Thanksgiving dinner. I was very anxious because we were late for the dinner and he was moving slower than molasses.

Suddenly, he started telling me how special it was that we parked in the same place where our souls would be joined as one very soon. He took my hand and said, "Esther, would you marry me?" He could barely finish before he started to cry. I couldn't believe it. I then saw him pulling out a box from the middle compartment of the car. I was sure it was the ring I gave him to use "whenever he was ready for this moment." I opened the box and found the most beautiful diamond ring I have ever seen. I never cried like that before.

Letting go of the expectation helped make this moment even more powerful. We were married on Dec. 24, 2008. You could feel all the love of the guests, friends and everyone who was involved in making this event so great.

Lessons from the Light

I learned to never give up on my dreams. I always visualize what I want and go after it. I must be patient and work on my own growth, working to be the best I can be. I don't waste time trying to change others. I learned that the Universe wants to give me everything. Once I got clear on what I wanted, I began to work toward it one step at a time. I realized that certainty is the most important feeling I could and should have. I also realized that every happy, sad and painful step of the way is necessary to help me learn certain lessons. Life is not about living it safe, it's about living with passion.

Biography

Esther considers herself first and foremost a spiritual being on a human journey. She has studied the Kabbalah for eight years and says it transformed her whole life. She is involved in community projects that are creating global change in the world. One main project is Spiritually for Kids, which works to empower the human spirit in every child. It teaches children to find their voices and make conscious choices that end the cycle of conflict for themselves and for future generations. Esther runs her own holistic facial business using ancient spiritual wisdom to awaken true beauty from within, combining mediation and spiritual tools throughout the experience.

Esther Levy

786-210-6057
esther10levels@yahoo.com
www.treeoflifefacials.com

Chapter Fourteen

PC McCullough

Favorite Quote

"Life is about the people you meet along the way."—PC McCullough

Passion

My life passion is to live life with passion!

Darkest Hour

I believe it's a good day when nobody dies. I am among the lucky baby boomers. I have two living parents who are still married to each other and who still function (albeit at a slower pace) on their own. Mom is a cancer survivor for 10-plus years now and Dad's 82 years are beginning to manifest in health issues, but certainly nothing that has stopped him from taking his daily walks and enjoying weekly card games. I am especially blessed with two loving, healthy children, each with their own sweet families and careers that give them a sense of value and financial stability. And so, at 58 years old, I am fortunate to have lived what I consider a good life.

My life, however, has not been without challenges. In 2008, I faced obstacles that heavily tested my belief in my strength to overcome. Just when my life was reaching its high point – in a loving relationship after more than 10 years of divorce, semi-retired in Florida, and living my dream of writing with the man of my dreams – the sands shifted. Hard times put a strain on the relationship and a dark cloud has loomed overhead since, so much so that there was a brief time when I questioned my purpose to the Universe. I still grieve the loss of a relationship I thought could and would withstand any challenge and cannot fathom the strength of the forces that were strong enough to pull us apart.

The year was tumultuous and the loss painful. But in the darkness, there is always light. My journals have been a source of strength in hard times. That strength has helped me adopt the attitude that guides me through life.

Lessons from the Dark

Today, I share a journal entry that was a turning point during this rocky time:

Sunday, December 7, 2008 – 9:45 AM Pearl Harbor Day

...Wow!! I just typed "most days I'm confused about where my life is going." As I read it, I realize I'm not at all confused about where my life is going. I just am not enjoying the ride right now. Life may be a roller coaster, but the thrills of life are at the top. I have never known anyone to raise their hands overhead in hair-raising anticipation of life's downward spirals. I'm no different. Well, maybe I am a little different. I discovered a few things on the way down life's roller coaster that some never find:

- My bootstraps, and they're strong and tough just like I am. I have a tight grip on them and I'm climbing.
- My two favorite books, *The Prophet* by Kahlil Gibran and *God on a Harley* by Joan Brady, an odd combination and both so meaningful in my life.
- Lessons from the past—sometimes you have to relive them to recall them.
  - Sometimes you have to relive them to recall them.
  - One person cannot make plans for two people.
  - Good people sometimes make bad decisions.
  - The person who they are is the person who they are.

- o   Accept and appreciate others but don't let them control you.
- o   It is what it is.
- o   Never make decisions in a time of crisis.
- Lessons for the future.
  - o   The one person you can always count on is yourself.
  - o   The other person you can always count on is your dog.
  - o   Look inside yourself and out to the Universe to find the answers to all your questions.
  - o   Sometimes it takes literally everything you have to become everything you want to be. Go for it, you are worth it!
  - o   Never lose sight of your dreams and set goals to reach them.
  - o   When you put all your eggs in one basket, be sure it's your basket.
  - o   The cream always rises to the top. I'll see you there!

Brightest Hour

At 30,000 feet, the clouds resembled banks of freshly fallen snow left behind in New England. Crammed into a window seat on an overcrowded airplane leaves little to look at, and I stared into the distance where the clouds met the sky. Several slow and deep breaths later, my mind drifted to the event I had witnessed just three hours earlier at Newton-Wellesley Hospital in Boston, Mass., when I watched my daughter comfort her newborn son, Colin Michael. Her second child, Colin joined our family just two days prior.

In the wee hours before dawn, I watched as she snuggled him into position for his feeding. For a brief moment her eyes met mine. They were filled with the love that only exists between mother and child, and I watched in awe of my baby girl whom I held lovingly in my arms for the first time nearly 35 years ago. The little girl who has brought such joy to my life is again a mother in her own right – loving and beautiful.

The two made a connection and the moments that followed were peaceful bliss. For that time there were no worries, no bills to pay, no wars, no national crises or economic turmoil, just pure and unconditional love – love that transcends romantic love, deep and boundariless – love that begins at conception and spans a lifetime and beyond.

My mind snapped a picture of the moment and sent it directly to my heart where it lives forever. I kissed them both and thanked God for the blessing.

Lessons from the Light

It is easy to become lost in negative thought. I have heard the expression, "In life there are moments of happiness." I refuse to believe that we were put on this Earth for a life of misery sprinkled with happy moments. Think positive thoughts and positive results will flow. Our lives are interspersed with challenges and pain that hold lessons to help us grow. Blessings are all around us and our good life is only as good as we make it. Beauty and happiness are disguised in everyday occurrences. Pay attention to every moment and be open to its message.

Biography

PC McCullough can find a story in the simplest of situations. Her writing can help us make sense of our personal conflicts. PC is dynamic, always changing and growing. Her ability to adapt, grow, and change will keep her in the forefront of authors who help us understand ourselves, what drives us, what we love and what we fear. PC published her first novel, *Perfect*, and is currently working on her second novel and a memoir. She is a career development coach and trainer, a life enthusiast, and recipient of the 2008 Vibrant Woman Award.

PC McCullough

New Life Essentials, LLC
for interviews or speaking engagements
1pcmccullough@gmail.com
newlifeessentialsllc@gmail.com
772.233.7675

Chapter Fifteen

Regena Ozeryansky

Favorite Quote

"In the shadow of the mountain of FEAR, lies the golden city of OPPORTUNITY."—Anonymous

Passion

I used to ask myself this question often, wondering what brings me the most joy. It showed up often in my life as loving and laughing. I love to smile and even when my face doesn't show it, my heart's passion is laughter and love. My life's purpose is to continue to love people and show others how to love more deeply.

Darkest Hour

I remember eight hours, eight dark, cold, lonely, sad, angry, confusing, vengeful, depressing, hateful hours. I remember sitting in my car frustrated and scared because I didn't know who I was. I had been driving for eight hours, searching for someone who clearly didn't want or know how to be with me. I couldn't even be with me...and I wanted this person to be with me?

It was dark, I was cold, I was scared and I was angry, *not at him, but at me.*

I was angry because "it" wouldn't go away. The fear, the hate, the anger, the suffering, the demon of my pain wouldn't go away. I had no clue how I had gotten myself to this point of disgust.

I remember looking down at my hands and wondering, who was this ugly person in my body? The vibrations in my hand increased as I examined my skin, which I no longer recognized. My hands were cold, and hot, and coarse and I wanted to cut them off. I couldn't imagine this was me who hated myself and others so much. I was pulling my hair and stomping my feet and screaming, and crying and I knew everyone must have heard, and still I felt nobody cared. I began rocking myself back and fourth, and back and fourth.

I had been hoping I could calm myself down, because I was too embarrassed to ask anyone to do it for me. Besides, I had gotten myself into this mess and I believed at the time that it was me who had to dig myself out of it. The rocking worked just long enough for 60 seconds to pass on the clock as I stared at it, waiting for it to turn to the next minute. The minute felt like hours, and the hours felt like months. I realized if I could do it for a minute, eventually I would get tired and fall asleep, and sure enough I did.

Lessons from the Dark

I was 19 years old at the time, and I believed that the key to love was giving up who I was. I learned after several sad and painful years that the only person who had the key to my heart was me. I learned that until I loved myself enough to care for me, there was absolutely no one who could do it for me. I had to nurture my needs before someone else's, and so I began to slowly pick myself up one piece at a time. I learned how to ask for what I needed, how to nurture myself and give to "Regena" what she deserved, which is what we all need—L-O-V-E!

Brightest Hour

Like a shining star that glows brighter and brighter the more you stare, I believe I too continue to shine in abundance and light. It is at this moment, right now, that I believe the brightest hour lies. Every moment that I am present, open and honest with myself I shine more brightly. I shine more brightly for those around me, for the universe, and for myself. I shine for humanity and equality and love. I shine for suffering, and fear and pain. I shine for those who have difficulty seeing their light as did I at many points in my journey. It is a true belief of mine, that we are each here to exist as one, and it is our right to help one another shine more bright one by one! Aho! (Native Lakota teaching that means "and so it is!")

Lessons from the Light

What I continue to learn is that life is ever changing, and there is no constant. And that is beautiful! I've learned to L-O-V-E, enjoy, and honor change as a gift of growth and inspiration. To remind me that journey and my lessons learned have pegged another point for someone else's growth.

Biography

Regena moved to South Florida from Maryland 5 years ago. With a passion for community and people, she entered the Real Estate industry and began helping people with their real estate goals and dreams. Keller Williams Realty, a national real estate firm, fueled her interest to become an active participant in the community. In 2007, Regena was named Rookie Realtor of The Year by the Realtor Association of Greater Fort Lauderdale. A love of people and community sparked her involvement with another amazing organization, Conscious Living Partnership, a powerful and inspiring company that helps educate people about global health and wellness. She is a founding member and president of the Ft. Lauderdale Chapter. With a unique blend of compassion and creativity, Regena continues to serve the community and universe with full intention of a better world.

Regena Ozeryansky
Keller Williams Realty
Direct: 786-286-8127
Rozeryansky@kw.com
www.EasyHomeMatch.com

Chapter Sixteen

Sheryl Olguin Paige

Favorite Quote

"Throughout the world sounds one long cry from the heart of the artist: give me the chance to do my very best."—Achille Papin
(from Isak Denisen's *Babette's Feast*, a film by Gabriel Axel)

Passion

I am a creative artist. For me, this takes expression in my career as a performing songwriter, as well as in my roles as producer and artist coach. Connecting with the audience in my performances completely energizes me. In addition to songwriting and performing, I am passionate about helping other artists and songwriters develop their abilities and personal expression. As a producer of audio and digital media, I love to capture the essence of an artist or business in a form that enables them to connect with their audience or clients.

Darkest Hour

My struggle began when I was diagnosed with an aggressive form of Non-Hodgkin's Lymphoma, a cancer of the lymphatic system. Lying in the hospital on a morphine drip to relieve the intense pain, I talked with God about my own mortality and eternity. My mind raced with thoughts of my husband, daughter, family and friends. In the solitary hours of those first nights, I lay there with tears streaming down my face thinking about how grateful I am to have them in my life. I realized how blessed my life has been.

A friend from church referred me to an oncologist, Dr. Sprawls. He answered my many questions and we got to know each other. I was battling fears of leaving my husband and daughter behind if I died. He asked me, "Are you afraid?" "Yes," I confessed through my tears. He calmly assured me that most of our fears are of the unknown, and encouraged me to get as informed as possible. So I set about the task of educating myself.

My treatment regimen was to last for months. My husband Leon and I quickly realized that we were going to need help, so he put the word out to our spiritual, musical, and business communities. Receiving from others has always been hard for me, but the circumstances forced me to put aside my pride and learn how to gratefully receive. We were flooded with offers to help in every conceivable way, from organizing fundraisers and financial help to bringing us meals and staying with me while Leon was out working. There has been so much help and kindness shown to me and my family that it would fill an entire book. A writer for the local newspaper interviewed me and commented that it must feel really good to know how loved you are in your own lifetime. "You have no idea," was all I could tell her.

My mother flew out from California for the start of my treatments. I was overwhelmed by countless medical appointments, tests, and growing piles of insurance paperwork. I remarked, "being sick is a full-time job." Mom corrected me. "No...getting WELL is a full-time job." This was an important shift of focus, because chemotherapy and its side effects are not fun. My sleep was disrupted, I had problems eating, I experienced emotional swings, my energy was gone and I lost my hair. I turned to my friend Kelly Palace for help developing an Olympic-level athlete's mindset to cope with the discomfort of my treatments. I was determined to beat this.

It wasn't long before I made a crucial realization. Every day I woke up alive I could choose how I would face that day. I decided that I would live, hope, love, and trust. I would *live* each day, hour, or moment, whatever that meant on that particular day. I would focus on *hope*. I would *love* each person I came in contact with and be sure that every experience would be positive. I would *trust* that ultimately God has my best interest at heart and deeply loves me. Nearly five months after the beginning of this ordeal, I received an excellent prognosis.

Lessons from the Dark

Keep focused on the positive, and each day to choose to live, hope, love and trust. Manage fears by getting informed and making informed decisions. I learned to sift out what is really important to me, and will begin putting my life back together from the ground up with a sense of focus I've never had before. It took facing my darkest hour to realize that some qualities simply can't be learned, they must be earned, forged into our being through personal experience.

Brightest Hour

The Harris/PBS DTV Express was the most fun I ever had in a corporate job, a once in a lifetime opportunity. I had been working at Harris Corporation for over 10 years, and had ridden the emergence of the Internet into roles as leader of a Web Development Center of Excellence, and leader of the corporate team Infobahn that dealt with Internet implementations, presence, policies and opportunities.

When the FCC mandated the transition from analog to digital television, Harris Corporation and PBS partnered to launch a 50-city nationwide educational tour to inform broadcasters about every aspect of the coming transition. Both companies knew that if the transition to digital were to be successful, broadcasters would need to know how to make it happen. They intended to be at the forefront of the transition, and wanted to create good will with broadcasters. The tour was the way to make that happen. I was selected for the project because I had the ability to quickly learn a technology and understand its potential applications, and the new DTV standard allowed Internet-like applications and data transmission over the air.

It was a thrilling time for me, working in a team of capable self-starters who really cared about creating a great outcome. Nobody punched a time clock. We worked from our homes, from hotel-rooms on the road, and in temporary offices as a virtual team. This was a group of people who really understood the value of teamwork. Looking back, I think I felt an excitement akin to what the engineers at NASA must have felt when getting the directive from JFK to go to the moon.

From the beginning, I determined to soak up as much knowledge and experience as possible. I learned many successful negotiation strategies from Jud French, executive director from Harris Corp., as well as how to create strategic alliances. Our project managers taught me the value of planning, managing risks, and understanding scope and costs. We managed to build a blended culture that drew from the best of both organizations.

We fielded a semi truck with a tractor-trailer that expanded "double-wide" that was a fully functional digital broadcast station in one half, and a consumer living room in the other half. We had a tour bus customized for the traveling crew with a mobile office and network. I represented Harris on the Advanced Television Systems Committee (ATSC) DASE subcommittee, an international voluntary non profit-organization that defined the technical standards for enhanced interactive digital television. This enabled me to understand the capabilities and applications that would be possible as this technology rolled out. I negotiated deals for broadcast and computer equipment donations and discounts, and outfitted our team with laptops and servers. I worked on demonstrations of interactive TV and data-casting used in the truck and shown at the National Association of Broadcasters (NAB) convention in Las Vegas. I was a technical adviser and integral part of the production team. This included the development and filming of "Bill Nye the Digital Guy," explaining how Digital and High Definition TV work.

Occasionally a friend contemplating the purchase of an HDTV or a DTV converter box will kid me accusingly, "this is your fault." I just smile, because I know that in a small way, it is.

Lessons from the Light

Change is inevitable, and you can embrace it and make things happen rather than simply letting things happen to you. Surround yourself with successful, capable people, and learn as much as you can from each one. Bringing your creativity into every aspect of work makes work fun.

Biography

For 13 years, Sheryl worked at Harris Corporation as a software developer, Internet team leader, and as the manager of DTV software and data technology. She left Harris to join her husband in their company, S.O.L.O. Creative Media, as V.P. of Production. She is a performing songwriter, using the stage name Sheryl Paige, and has five releases, and multiple songwriting awards to her credit. She coaches artists and songwriters, from nationally touring artists to beginners. Sheryl is the regional coordinator for central Florida MAMAPALOOZA events, providing a stage for women to showcase their talents. In addition, she is the co-coordinator of the NSAI songwriters chapter in Orlando. In 2008 Sheryl was selected as the ABWA Woman of the Year (Oceanside Charter Chapter).

Sheryl Olguin Paige

Sheryl@solocreativemedia.com
Sheryl@sherylpaige.com
www.sherylpaige.com
www.solocreativemedia.com

Chapter Seventeen

Kelly Palace, M. Ed.

Favorite Quote

"It is better to execute a good plan than to never execute the perfect plan."—General Patton

Passion

Personal development and leadership are my passions. There is nothing more rewarding than watching someone develop or evolve as a person, and it is even more rewarding when I have a hand in helping someone grow. Leadership, as I see it, involves demonstrating on a consistent basis outstanding qualities in oneself as an inspiration to others. An equally powerful definition of Leadership is that it is the combination of vision and urgency.

Darkest Hour

It was a morning with "abundant sunshine," as our weather channel describes most days in South Central Florida. Even better, it was our wedding anniversary and life was good. This was the thought I had just moments before I was confronted by two uniformed police officers and a plain clothes "female" detective standing before me. "Are you Kelly

Palace?" the female asked me. I nodded. "You are under arrest for ..." (I must stop here and tell you that for this moment time stood still. I quickly scanned my mind: Unpaid parking tickets? None. Unpaid taxes? None. Having a dirty shower? Wait, they don't arrest people for that. What on earth could I have done?! I had NEVER had an incident with the law, except a speeding ticket. I am an honest, law abiding, good citizen, a community volunteer and leader. Why was I being arrested? It must be a mistake!) "...Insurance Fraud," the detective finished her sentence. "Insurance Fraud?!" I couldn't believe it. I knew this was a mistake and it must be that someone had stolen my identity and I was being arrested instead of her! This was truly my first conclusion. I was sure I had been done in by an identity thief.

The day got worse. On the 45 minute ride to the county jail, my arms went numb because they were handcuffed so tightly behind my back. I rode in shocked silence and disbelief. Then I was booked into the county jail, my clothes were taken and I was re-dressed in cinder-block-gray scrubs, minus undies, and plastic flip-flops, for a long day of being locked up in an ice cold cell. I was trembling the entire day, freezing cold. Later I would understand my body was in a medical "state of shock." Eventually the news of my arrest hit the front page of the newspaper, after all, I was a community leader. The 10 months between the time when I was arrested and when my case was dropped were a nightmare. This was a felony charge with the possibility for a 15 year sentence. Innocent people do get convicted, my nightmare's fodder.

How did this happen? Almost a year before my arrest, I was receiving "disability pay" for OCD and Panic disorder while employed for a large Fortune 500 corporation. I hated being on disability, but my doctor ordered me to do so. This episode of panic attacks came because my stress level was at its peak. Within a six month period I had gotten divorced, changed jobs, gotten re-married, moved and was in a near miss high speed car collision. At this point, I couldn't get behind the wheel of a car without having a panic attack. It was a good thing I was on disability-it wasn't safe for me or you, if I had driven. Hence, I couldn't work (I was a Pharmaceutical Rep who spent eight hours a day in a car). I was only on disability pay for a few months. At the time of my arrest, I had been off disability for seven months and was fully recovered.

I have suffered, on and off throughout my life, with OCD, Panic and Depression (mostly OCD and Panic). I have been treated by doctors, taken medications, received counseling, changed jobs, ended relationships and consciously chosen not to have children, all because of my mood disorders. I have tried to hide my disorder out of embarrassment and shame.

Why was I arrested? My insurance company wanted their money back on the claim they had paid me for those few months. They withheld medical evidence from the State when they filed criminal charges against me. With my long history of mood disorder, can you imagine them NOT sending my medical records to the prosecuting attorney when they filed charges? The insurance company wanted the "claim reversed" and they do it everyday, no matter how much harm it causes someone, all to maximize their profits. In their arrest report they claimed I had been "faking," that I "wasn't psychologically disabled."

It was a very dark hour for me when I was accused of a crime; but even darker and more horrible, was, after all of those years of trying to hide my disability, to be publicly exposed and humiliated by having my story spread across the front page of the newspaper.

The action of the insurance company in disrespecting my disability and misleading law enforcement for financial gain was a violation of everything I hold sacred. My character was assassinated, my good name and reputation ruined, and the very foundation of my world was yanked out from under me. I was snubbed by neighbors, heckled in the grocery store, and the target of many months of a hateful email campaign waged by a member of the media (who later apologized). Just as a victim violated in a carnal rape cannot convey the depths of their despair and horror of the event--so I cannot communicate to you the psychological damage and devastation that the insurance company caused me. And, for what? Greed! A friend suggested it was like being murdered and then living to tell about it. Besides the obvious, emotional and financial damages, the immediate stress reaction after the arrest was for my body to break out in severe eczema, from head to toe that put me in "itching hell" and gave me unsightly skin for over a year.

If you want more clarity on my case, fire up your DVD player and pop in the movie SICKO, a documentary on the Health Care Industry. It explains my case clearly. Check out Scenes 2-4 and finish with "The Hit Man" where they interview a former claims agent for a large insurance company. His name is Lee Einer. Lee's most memorable (and most-quoted) line in SICKO: "You're not slipping through the cracks. Somebody made that crack and swept you towards it. And the intent is to maximize profits." He goes on to say, "I'm not proud of what I did. Did I kill anyone? Nah. Did I do harm in peoples' lives? Hell yeah!" Lee gives a very dark insight into what some insurance companies do to innocent people so they can maximize profits. I was an innocent victim,100 percent innocent.

When the prosecuting attorney finally saw my medical history, which the insurance company had concealed, they dropped the case. Dropped - not tried, not negotiated, not reduced. Dropped! I don't blame the State for arresting me. I blame my insurance company for misleading law enforcement to maximize profits. I don't think they wanted me behind bars— I think they wanted the leverage of saying, "If you pay us back, we will drop these charges." Thank goodness the State's Attorney could see through this tactic. For that, I am grateful.

Lessons from the dark

There is no greater asset than friends and family in a time of need. In my dark hours of this horrific event I was shown the meaning of true love and friendship! A community of friends rallied around me: supported, loved and protected me. My family and friends came from around the country to support me. They gave me love and strength. My amazing husband was a rock for me, providing unwavering support and love.

Additionally, I feel a lesson for me is to "shine the light" on this disorder and how, at times, it can be a real disability. I was able to hire an excellent Criminal Attorney (Richard Canina, Melbourne, Florida) to go through the stacks of paperwork and figure out that my medical file was missing from the prosecuting attorney's file. What about others, who aren't so fortunate? I still suffer with mood disorders, at times, but I can be an example for others living with OCD or Panic that one still live a fulfilling life as I have. Yes, there are times when it can knock you down, but getting back up is the cure.

Final lesson from this darkness: don't always believe what you read or see in the media. The inaccuracy with which the media covered my case was mind-boggling. The "sensationalizing" of my story was all they were interested in, not the facts. What was printed in the newspaper was barely recognizable as my case. The breaking news story about me was on the front page with my photo. The story of my case being dropped was buried in the back pages with no photo.

My Brightest Hour

My brightest hour is always when I am pursuing a worthy goal or assisting someone in achieving his or her worthy goal, when I am working in conjunction with others to achieve a common goal, like working with great women on this book. There is nothing brighter or more energizing than to be passionate about a goal. Fortunately, these bright moments can come in the form of both the pursuit and the achievement of our goals.

I have had many goals that have evoked my passion and driven me forward in the face of great obstacles. The first goal I remember setting was to break swimming records in our "summer league" championships at the age of 9. I went on to set many swimming performance goals, some of which I achieved and some I did not. One example of a goal I did not achieve but provided an incredible journey was to make a United States Olympic Team in swimming. While I never did this, the journey to this goal provided me with some other amazingly bright hours, such as earning a full athletic swimming scholarship to college, setting many state and national swimming records, earning NCAA All-American honors, Olympic Trial Standards and traveling to great places for swim meets and training.

While I "fell short" of making the Olympic Team, I would never have accomplished many wonderful things without that lofty goal. While all of this might sound easy, looking back on it, I was up at 4:30 am most mornings of high school and 5:30 am in college to reach these goals. Without passion and conviction for going to the Olympics, I would probably have just rolled over and gone back to sleep on those many mornings. Instead, I hit the cold water and averaged seven miles swimming a day. This was a routine I kept for 15 years. And what bright hours they were. Through swimming I met my two best friends in the world Beth and Nancy, bright, shining, lifelong friends.

Throughout my life, I have used goal setting as an important aspect of creating bright moments. After swimming, I went into college coaching and was the only woman division one swimming coach in the Southeastern Conference for 10 years, where I was impassioned by helping my athletes and teams achieve their goals. What a journey this was! Again, I fell short of many goals but achieved much, including watching 24 of my swimmers earn NCAA All-American Honors. Ten of them made Olympic Trials Standards and our team had the best grade point average of all Division I team's in the nation. Again brightly, I made more lifelong friendships.

Of course, my brightest hour is ALWAYS today; this moment, moving toward a worthy goal. My vision and passion energize me today to provide leadership to others looking for inspiration and a way to evolve, develop as a person and live life at one's highest level.

Lessons from the brightness

It really is the journey, not the destination, that one needs to enjoy on the way to his or her dream or goal. If you make the journey fun, exciting and where you want to be, then you are "living the dream." Too many of us live on "someday I'll," cleverly renamed "Someday Isle." Go for it now, not after you lose 20 pounds, or get out of debt, or get your degree, or find the right partner. We are ready for our best lives now, right now!

Biography

Kelly Palace is a community leader, sought-after speaker and businesswoman who created a "million dollar product" that has been sold in 9 countries around the world. After 20 years in corporate America, Kelly found her entrepreneurial spirit and launched several successful businesses and products. She is the founder and director of the Annual Vibrant Women's Conference. Kelly is an advocate for promoting women-owned businesses and empowering women through personal and professional development. She is especially passionate about volunteering for Zonta and bringing awareness to Human Trafficking. Book Kelly to speak at your next event at www.KellyPalace.com.

Kelly Palace, M. Ed.

321-773-5611
KellyPalace@earthlink.net
www.VibrantCareer.com
www.VibrantWomensConference.com
www.KellyPalace.com
www.VibrantWomensWisdom.com

Chapter Eighteen

Maria P. Parker

Favorite Quote

"They that hope in the Lord will renew their strength, they will soar as with eagles wings. They will run and not grow weary, walk and not grow faint."— Isaiah 40:31

Passion

Running has been an important part of my adult life. I have seen firsthand how regular exercise lifts the spirits and helps to improve mental and physical health. I have literally run away from my problems only to find myself stumbling to their solutions. I am currently working on a degree in counseling, which I plan to combine with my passion for exercise to develop a counseling practice based on exercise.

Darkest Hour

Sitting in my counselor's office with my husband, I couldn't believe the words coming out of his mouth. He was leaving me. He wanted to tell me there, because he knew I would be emotional, perhaps angry and dangerous. He wanted the counselor around to console me, and to pick up the pieces if necessary. As he left me sitting in her office 10 minutes later, I did fall apart. Literally, falling to the floor wailing. I'd tried to be the perfect wife for five months since the horrible January day a friend told me she thought my husband was having an affair. I'd struggled to be even better than the perfect wife I was sure I had been for the previous 23 years. But he was leaving me anyway, for a beautiful, skinny 24-year-old blond.

It was all so lurid and cliché, like a really awful soap opera. It was surreal in that it was my own and every middle-aged woman's worst nightmare. In my pride, I felt I'd done everything right. I'd worked hard to raise our four children, even homeschooling them for most of their education. I'd stayed fit and attractive, read many books on how to be a good wife. I even had sex with my husband anytime he wanted.

When I found out about the affair, I was incredulous. It had been going on for 10 months under my nose and at times, in my own bed. I felt foolish, angry, and desperate to make it all go away. I told him if he ended it right away, I would forgive him and we could put it back together.

He did try to end it with her, but vacillated over the next five months between the two of us. Eventually he was unable to shake his attraction for this woman and the life of love, fun and admiration she promised him.

He finally decided he wanted what she offered and didn't think I could ever forgive him for the affair anyway. That day in the counselor's office he moved on to the next phase of his life.

I grieved and cried and lost weight and sleep. All the while he seemed content and relieved. He assured me he loved me as the mother of his children and wanted to have a good relationship with me. He moved in with her. I became the bitter, jilted wife and let everyone in the community know what an awful thing he'd done to me. I was ugly and miserable.

The darkest part of it was lying awake night after night with pain in my chest and a voice inside my head screaming, *Why?* I got little consolation from my faith, and even less from the well-meaning encouragement I received to move on and find a new man. I felt like someone had reached inside me and ripped something out.

As the months went by, we both hired attorneys, he moved his clothing and computer out and we moved inexorably toward becoming another divorce statistic.

Lessons from the Dark

It slowly dawned on me that I'd had a part in the failure of our marriage. During the heart-aching nights I realized I'd rarely put Jim first. I'd filled my life with community activities that challenged me. I loved the admiration of my friends and neighbors. But I left Jim alone many evenings, and would thoughtlessly put him down in front of the children and others. The lessons from the sadness were about my pride. As I tried to do everything "right," I had begun to believe I was better than he was. I had forgotten to be loving, humble and soft with my best friend.

Brightest Hour

Knowing you've made a mistake doesn't make it better, but is the bottom rung of a ladder that leads somewhere better. After a couple of months, though I believed that my marriage was over, I made a choice to forgive Jim for his affair, and asked him to forgive me for the part I had played in the demise of our relationship. We both fired our attorneys and hired a mediator who would work with us to create an equitable settlement of our assets. I stopped complaining about Jim to my friends and family and I began to feel more peaceful and optimistic about my future. I enrolled in a master's degree program to become a Licensed Professional Counselor and threw myself into my athletic pursuits. I did half-marathons, a full marathon, a triathlon, and a weeklong 500-mile bike ride. I cut down on my community activities and tried to simplify my life as much as possible. The exercise and new plan for my future helped rebuild my self-confidence.

Meanwhile, the luster of Jim's relationship with his girlfriend was beginning to tarnish. He was unsure of what to do. He moved out of his girlfriend's apartment into his own place, though he continued seeing her. At the same time, we began to get to know one another again. We had many long discussions about our past and slowly, his affection for me began to return. We learned about a retreat for couples whose marriages were deeply troubled and signed up for it. At the same time, we finished our separation agreement with the mediator.

During the retreat we learned about communicating feelings and practical ways to rebuild our relationship. The most important thing we discovered was that other couples had gone through similar circumstances and their marriages had survived and thrived.

However, Jim remained ambivalent and three weeks later I finally decided that there was no hope for our marriage. I told him I was moving on. My decision changed something in Jim and that same heart-rending afternoon, he decided to be completely honest with me. He revealed everything about his secret life during our marriage and since he'd left me. He showed me letters, pictures and e-mails between him and his girlfriend. He gave me the freedom to ask any questions I had, and answered them fully and honestly. Finally, on his knees he begged my forgiveness and asked me to move in with him and stay with him forever.

In those hours, my heart and our marriage were reborn. I gratefully accepted the second chance to love him. In the last nine months I have experienced more joy than I have in the last 45 years of my life. We have both learned to love each other more effectively. It took Jim's affair to break through my pride and help me become a more loving person. It took Jim's affair to help him learn to communicate his feelings and become truly open with me for the first time in our lives together.

Lessons from the Light

Wonderful things can and do come from awful things. Our reconciliation has taught me thankfulness. Each day I feel grateful to have Jim in my life and my family whole again. I am inspired to appreciate all the little things that make my life good. I've learned to be less judgmental and dogmatic and to worry about the plank in my own eye before attending to the speck in another's eye. Finally, we've both learned that the power of forgiveness is limitless. We forgave each other and ourselves and enjoy the peace and joy of that each day.

Biography

Maria P. Parker is a wife and mother of four children. She owns a bicycle business, with her husband and is working on her master's degree in counseling. She enjoys all forms of exercise, especially running and cycling.

Maria P. Parker

910-739-2400
mparker27@gmail.com

Chapter Nineteen

Rev. Jann Rossbach

Favorite Quote

"Love gives us in a moment what we can hardly attain by effort after years of toil."—Johann Wolfgang Von Goethe

Passion

I am energized and "plugged in" to what I feel is my purpose on Earth when I am appreciating and creating beauty. This can involve painting a picture, or creating a dream-catcher, or writing a poem, or presenting a class to help others connect more deeply to Source and sense their own form of empowerment. I am passionate about relating heart to heart as I share healing touch in bodywork sessions. I am passionate as I breathe in wonder and awe to experience the beauty of life. My life's passion is to extend love and compassion to all beings.

Darkest Hour

Times of "darkness" can be uncomfortable and sad when loss in some form is upon us. A day before my partner of eight years was sent home to die, I bought a tape recorder and I recorded myself telling myself to "remember that good things *are* happening." I would play that recording back to myself as I was immersed in witnessing his suffering and self-torture.

I was blessed to have a circle of friends so loving, who surrounded me in a time when my reality felt like a nightmare of pain and lies and rage. I meditated and decided to purposely shift my focus to better-feeling thoughts no matter what was happening around me. When I could not do that, I looked around for something to appreciate. I decided to be easier with myself and to trust that a greater plan, orchestrated by a loving Higher Power, *was* unfolding in my life.

Forces of destruction and death challenge me to the very core of my being. At the core is Divine Love, a breath of fresh air, a fuller acceptance of me.

In the darkest hours, I am compelled to connect with the Light of Source. When I allow that connection I have discovered treasures that are stored within me.

Perhaps the darkness serves to drive me more honestly into greater understanding and trust of this; *All* things come together for the good of humanity.

Even in suffering and pain, Love is loving through me.

Though I may be tossed into darkness and feel like I can't get a grip, there *is* something in all the confusion that will guide me to trust even more. "Dark nights of the soul" can be an opportunity for me to go deeper, beneath lies and labels to find stillness and soothing relief. For in times of darkest hours an honest observance of me has helped me to shed old beliefs full of dread so that, in time, I come to see that in cycles of daylight and darkness I live in a place of beauty.

Aho!

Lessons from the Dark

Passage into Darkness

This passage into darkness cycles once again,
And here I go.....
And *how* I go determines the jolt of the spin.

In times of loss and challenge, when I've run fearful into me,
the view I have seems limited
as I blame and judge myself unworthy.

A pattern, a habit, a sense of despair attracts more of the same
and unless I can choose to see beyond, I'm held securely in the victim
game.
Yet, when I find myself in the dark, if I open up just a bit
to relax and release the grip of grief
I begin to take in Divine Guidance and connect with Source in me.

For darkness has its blessings just waiting to be revealed
and as I dive into secret chambers,
I sense compassion.
I *am* being healed.

Throughout my life I have faced Darkest Hours and sensed hopelessness
yet still
as I decide to reach for a spark of relief,
fan the flames of Love and Creator's will,
Mercy and Grace flood into this place.

I can trust that the light will return.
For in these times of darkness the awareness's that I learn
serve to help me shed my false beliefs
and as I understand the Law that offers insights clear
I bless it all
Release it all
I'm grateful to be here.

Brightest Hour

"Recall lessons learned from your 'Brightest Hour' and your 'Darkest Hour' and write about them in order to share useful insights and practices with others." The challenge was exciting and I love to write! I decided, "I'm going to do this!" and so I began writing.

The first article I chose to write about, without hesitancy, was from my "darkest hour." Now, to write about my brightest hour! For some reason I feel discomfort. I've certainly experienced bright hours throughout my life!

"Hmmm, I'm trying to think of a good one."

I decided to list several bright moments in my life and then choose one to begin this "brightest hour" article. On a blank page entitled My Brightest Moment I looked at the word "Brightest" and I created an acronym:

Beautiful
Realizations
Ignite
Gracious
Honest
Thoughts
Establishing
Sacred
Thinking

"Stop right there!" I hear myself say. "You've just accessed an interesting insight into where *your* focus most easily tracks!"

Yes, I have!

I acknowledge, right now, that this discomfort that I am feeling is a result of how I *have* focused more on learning through pain than on learning through joy. Is *that* why I find it easier to write about lessons learned through struggle in my life?

I consider that this is a habit of thought for me, one that I'm not always aware of. I have believed that I deserve some level of punishment. This habit of thought is creating my experiences in life. Because of this, I act out in unconscious ways.

My personal desire is to become more aware and conscious of my patterns of thought that create resistance within me and that keep me from being in alignment with joy as I live my passion.

Today, I have experienced such awareness! I have experienced a deeper understanding about my "resistances" to abundant living. This is an opportunity for me to establish sacred thinking.

I would say that *this* is my brightest moment!

Lessons from the Light

I know that how I feel in the moment IS the vibration that I extend to be matched by the Universal Law of Attraction. Now that I'm aware of this habit of thought and have insight into my resistances, I can change my point of attraction!

Realization *is* a beautiful gift!

I feel empowered to shift my patterns of thought. The good news is that as I choose to experience brightness and joy *now* and then let it in, I am assured that more brightness and joy *is* the coming attraction!

As I am in a state of appreciation and eagerness to live my life's passion, I *am* in alignment with Divine Creator who desires to guide me into my highest good. This moment, Right here, right now, is a very Bright moment, indeed!

Biography

Rev. Jann Rossbach ~ Dancing Light (a name given me by spiritual "elders") has been involved in the healing arts profession for over 30 years. As a former RN now practicing as a Licensed Massage Therapist, Jann offers an eclectic range of modalities to extend healing touch. She manufactures a soothing and healing Arnica Salve. Jann is an ordained minister with the Universal Brotherhood Movement and serves as a volunteer at a local hospital in the spiritual care department. She enjoys creating ceremony and facilitating gatherings within her community that will uplift participants and celebrate the wonder, magnificence and connection that is afforded to all of us in this life. As the mother of three grown children, Jann has experienced a wealth of lessons learned through co-creating! She lives in Merritt Island, Fla.

Rev. Jann Rossbach

sacred_space_creations@yahoo.com
321-431-6359

Chapter Twenty

Nan Akasha, CHT

Favorite Quote

Our deepest fear is not that we are inadequate. Our deepest fear is that we are powerful beyond measure. It is our light, not our darkness that most frightens us. We ask ourselves, Who am I to be brilliant, gorgeous, talented, fabulous? Actually, who are you not to be? You are a child of God. Your playing small does not serve the world. There is nothing enlightened about shrinking so that other people won't feel insecure around you. We are all meant to shine, as children do. We were born to make manifest the glory of God that is within us. It's not just in some of us; it's in everyone. And as we let our own light shine, we unconsciously give other people permission to do the same. As we are liberated from our own fear, our presence automatically liberates others.—Marianne Williamson

Passion

My life's passion is fun. I love to really immerse myself in the now and experience life fully. I live life seeking extraordinary experiences and adventure, enjoying each sensation and discovering how to tune my energies to what feels best. Travel, inner world search, coaching and seeing clients have delicious breakthroughs all ignite my passion. I choose to make life fun, and then it is effortless. Passion is fueled by designing a life that enhances each moment. My deepest fulfillment comes when my inner work and breakthroughs combine with travel. Like going to a sacred or beautiful place like Egypt, and meditating with a group of people. It combines the new people, places and foods with personal growth. I soar.

Darkest Hour

I have had several of what I call life "deconstructions." You know, when everything in your world literally comes apart, and you do not know what is real anymore?

I believe my darkest hour is my most recent, even after I endured the death of my baby daughter after eight years of trying to get pregnant. For nearly three years, I waded through a surreal world of divorce. After 25 years, I finally got the courage to ask for a separation. My husband was depressed, resentful and uncommunicative, and the energy in my house was oppressive. I focused my time and energies on two things: my adopted twin daughters and my then-successful real estate investing business. I hated to be in the house, and could not get him to talk or go to counseling – until it was too late. I was terrified of hurting or angering him, so my guilt created a vortex of energy that sucked everything into a void, and dropped me out the bottom a few years later, exhausted, depleted and broken, financially and emotionally.

I had hoped for an amicable separation. I placed no blame and hate being in a victim mode, as it gets you nowhere but stuck in powerlessness. However, his anger and pain mixed with my guilt created a true personal hell. My ex began to accuse me of strange things like hiding money and threatened to "expose" me as a bad mother in court. He tried to get custody of my children, which nearly killed me, having had a daughter die and going through so much to adopt my twins. Soon I was in the hospital having tests because I literally could not eat. I was on medicine to calm a spastic stomach and lost weight at an unhealthy rate. My brain began to fog over as he blocked me from closing real estate deals and benefitting from the proceeds. He and his team of attorneys spied on me and killed business deals. Title companies refused to close deals, colleagues began to turn away and my reputation crashed. My attorney convinced me to file bankruptcy and other lawsuits began.

I sat in denial that my husband would do this, saying "but he is a nice person." I trusted him and negotiated directly with him, only to be shocked when my attorney would reveal some new court filing he had made behind my back while asking me to "just get it over with."

As my business, money and associates disappeared, so did my emotional support. My parents were very upset that I wanted a divorce and took his side. To this day they only speak to him, and only know his skewed perspective on the whole event. The last straw came when my mother came to my house and in front of my children and others screamed at me about how useless and horrible I was and that she wanted me out of the family. The cherry on top was her trying to hit me while yelling, "I don't love you, I don't love you, I don't love you anymore!" No money, no business, no family, no health...a dark hour indeed.

Lessons from the Dark

These moments of extreme emotional challenge are actually doorways to self-realization and personal freedom. They bless us with a chance to let go of what others think and allow us to go within to find our own strength and truth. My lesson: I cannot please anyone else, ever. I must be true to myself, follow my inner voice. We are all responsible for our own reality. We can choose how we feel, who we are, what we do. The gift is release from attachment, pain, and past. The power is shifting limiting beliefs. I found self-love and inner peace. It is a doorway to a richer, more authentic life, a doorway to our divine nature, and unconditional love.

Brightest Hour

My brightest hour is meeting and allowing-in the love of my life, my soul mate Chris. I met Chris eight months after my separation, but before the nightmare of the divorce began. I was not looking for anyone, yet I was truly blissful. I was happy, feeling free, powerful and full of possibility. I was creating my life in my own way for the first time in more than two years and I felt alive, young and happy. I began to "sense" him a month prior to meeting him. I felt someone was out there, and I did not know who. We met when he attended a talk I gave in real estate investing. He was quiet and reserved and I thought he had been dragged there. He would invite me to lunch with his dad and business partner every two weeks or so. Even though his father would talk all the time and he hardly spoke, we began to realize how much we had in common: travel, business, investing. Then we began to run into each other all over town. We discovered a shared interest in spirituality and prosperity consciousness. Law of attraction in action!

One day he invited me to a talk with a Hawaiian shaman. By now I had decided the intense energy I was picking up was definitely coming from him. Although he gave no indication that he was romantically interested in me, I had been taken over by the soul energy coming from him to my heart. After the dinner we stayed up until 6 a.m. in the hotel lobby talking. I finally decided to be brave and I hinted I was interested in him. It was like an electric shock had gone through him! He sat up, looked at me and said, "I'm interested." He told me later he was fascinated by me, but never thought I would be interested in him. I am so glad I followed the feelings within me, even though I did not understand them.

As we sat and held hands looking into each others eyes, my mind kept saying "kiss him." It terrified me because I had not kissed anyone but my ex-husband in over 28 years! The magnetic power of love between us was too strong though. I reached out and grabbed his jacket and pulled him to me. I kissed him, and we melted together.

We have been together for 2 ½ years. My life has not been the same since. I live every day with a man who appreciates me, allows me to be myself, supports me, loves me and is kind and generous. He is the best receiver ever. I can love him completely and never feel like he rejects my love. I stayed focused on "only unconditional love" through our time getting to know each other, and it was returned to me one thousand fold! I live in a love I never knew possible. I am so blessed I let him in.

Lessons from the Light

I now know that when we follow our bliss, we invite in our heart's desire. We must be what we want in our lives. When I met Chris I had gone through the fear of getting out of a 25- year marriage and I felt free. I was happy and full of love, joy and possibility. I felt that all things were possible and I was loving myself and valuing what I wanted for the first time. In this wonderful state I was able to tune in to his vibration and I followed my inner knowing. I trusted and decided to play full-out and take a chance. I chose to only see him with loving eyes and only do what I truly wanted, acting from unconditional love. This made my energy field ripe and open to receive this amazing love into my life experience.

Biography

Nan Akasha, CHT is a healing intuitive, belief-shifting expert, inner-power coach, teacher, author, speaker.

A firm believer in EXPERIENTIAL learning and personal freedom, Nan's ongoing, joyful transformational journey is to explore the deepest potential of our soul awareness, re-access our natural unlimited state of being and re-activate true prosperity in all areas. Nan uses her 20 years experience in a vast array of philosophies and healing and manifestation tools to clear limiting beliefs, open awareness, inspire passion and reveal personal purpose. Nan's passion is to design the easiest, most fun and effective tools for explosive healing, abundance and harmony in your life.

As an intensely happy human and a mother of twins, Nan creates original sourced tools, audios and classes to empower and assist you to design your unique success from the inside out.

Nan Akasha, CHT

Phone: 210-535-8239
Email: nan@CreateYourOwnRealityNow.com
Main Website: CreateYourOwnRealityNow.com
My other websites:
mymoneymuse.com
MagicPotionsforYou.com
IntuitionAccelerator.com
IntendGlobalHealing.com
UltimateAwarenessCoaching.com
AskYourMoneyMuse.com

Chapter Twenty-One

Mary Ellen Troilo

Favorite Quote

"The people who get on in this world are the people who get up and look for the circumstances they want, and, if they can't find them, make them."— *George Bernard Shaw*

Passion

I truly believe that the challenges, events and people that occur in our lives are part of a master plan. It's what we do as a result of these circumstances that will dictate whether that account is to be positive or negative. As a result of a tragic incident involving my mother, my life completing changed for the better. By wanting to give back to a community that had been there for her, I volunteered to educate women on personal finances. This has become one of the most rewarding aspects of my life and one that I am most passionate about.

Darkest Hour

My darkest hour occurred when my mother, who was 58, was shot in the back of the head and in the chest. I remember the day like it was yesterday. I received the call from my sister-in-law stating that Mom had been shot. All I could think was "He did it, he shot her!" I knew exactly who had done it. He had threatened her many times over the last 6 weeks. It was her ex-boyfriend.

They had had a good relationship and he seemed like a nice guy. I met him a couple of times over the years. At some point, however, Mom said he changed. He became angry at the simplest things, grew moody and wasn't nice to be around. Mom decided that she had had enough and didn't want to be around him anymore. She told him that she could be friends with him, but that was it. This seemed to make matters worse and he began to threaten her, follow her, show up in public places and taunt her.

My sister and I told her to get some advice from an attorney and to visit the local women's shelter. She did everything they advised her to do. She went to court four times in the 30 days before the shooting asking the court to grant her a restraining order due to the threats, stalking, threatening calls, etc. There wasn't sufficient evidence, according to the court. Not much was done.

I remember the flight with my brothers from Orlando, Fla., to Raleigh, N.C., when it first happened. I couldn't believe it. I was in shock. Things like this didn't happen to people like my mother. Would she survive the surgery? Would I be able to tell her how much I loved her one more time? Could I have done something more to help her and prevent this from happening? So many thoughts just kept going through my mind. It was one of the longest flights that I have ever taken. Not knowing if my mother would survive was the worst part.

My mother did survive the shooting. The doctors were amazed. She was in the hospital for six weeks. Her injuries resulted in a broken jaw from one of the bullets and a stroke from a nicked carotid artery. Her chest injury, although shot from close range, was minor. She had to learn how to speak, eat and walk again. After six months of therapy with speech, occupational and physical therapists, she remains with left-side paralysis and can no longer drive or be independent.

In the end, the judge who did not do anything for my mother was investigated after this incident. Her case was cited as an example of how lenient this judge was in cases that involved domestic violence. He has since stepped down from his position.

Mom's ex pleaded guilty and is serving a 22-year sentence without possibility of parole.

Lessons from the Dark

When it comes to domestic violence, a woman should not take ANY THREAT lightly, whether verbal or physical. No matter how well you know a person, if they become violent toward you in any way for whatever reason, consider how you would counsel a friend or sister in the same situation. Now take your own advice. Contrary to what you are told, it is not your fault and you don't deserve that type of treatment, EVER! Don't let your emotions rule your head. Take action to protect yourself.

Brightest Hour

My happiest hour was my college graduation. As I was waiting in the long line of other graduates to receive our diplomas, I had a few minutes to reflect on the previous four years it took to get to that point.

I had decided four years earlier that I wanted to complete my education. I wasn't sure how I was going to do it until one day my brother-in-law recommended that I try bartending. He told me about a position that was opening at one of the local sports bars. It was a popular spot and I knew that the bartenders were well paid, so I went in and was able to get an interview with the manager.

That day changed the rest of my life. I don't think I had ever been more nervous or out of place. Somehow I made it through the interview and as it came to a close, the manager asked me how to make a specific drink. I had no idea and told him so. I said if he would give me a chance, I would learn all of the drinks by the end of the week! He grinned at that and then said that if he hired someone with such little experience, his other bartenders would not be happy. He would have to fire me. So I told him that since he was a smart businessman, he should hire me and if I didn't work out, he could fire me in two weeks, no questions asked. I am not sure how that came out of my mouth, but I figured if I didn't speak up, I had no chance at all of getting that job. Well, he hired me for two weeks and I stayed for five years.

As each year passed and I got closer to finishing my degree, I used to joke with my customers that I was doing a psychology internship behind the bar. I am not sure what gave me a better education, the classes that I took during the day or bartending in the evening. In any event, my regular customers took care of me every night and they are partially responsible for financing my degree. In addition to the customers, my fellow bartenders and my manager did their part by being supportive and adaptable to my schedule.

During my last semester, however, I overbooked myself and grew very overwhelmed with my schedule of classes. I was nearing the end of my semester and couldn't handle it. I told a co-worker/friend that I was ready to quit. He convinced me to go to my manager and request some time off. In the end, my manager gave me 10 straight days off so I could finish my semester and graduate.

When I walked across the stage to receive my diploma, I looked up and in addition to my family, I saw 25 of my bar customers cheering me on. Now that is support!

Lessons from the Light

As I look back on my college days, the lesson that I learned was not to be afraid to ask for what you need or want. Everyone, at some point in their lives, will face challenges. It's how you react to those challenges that will shape your life. It's okay to admit that you can't do something and request the help you need. You may have to get out of your comfort zone, but don't be afraid to speak up and ask for it.

Biography

Mary Ellen was raised in Orlando, Fla., and went to college at the University of Central Florida. She graduated with a bachelor's degree in Psychology and Business. She entered the mortgage industry in 1994 and continued to educate herself on the industry, and continued to expand her mortgage practice. She specializes in educating clients in purchasing residential real estate, and in college, savings, retirement and divorce planning. She is the owner of Riverside Home Loans, Inc., a Correspondent Lender, located in Indialantic, Fla.

She lives in Indialantic, Fla., with her mother and two very spoiled dogs. She still maintains friendships with her bartender buddies from her college years.

Mary Ellen Troilo

321-726-0570
maryellen@riversideloans.net
www.MakeYourMillionwithME.com

Chapter Twenty-Two

Melodie D. Tucker

Favorite Quotes

"Life is not measured by the number of breaths we take, but by the moments that take our breath away."—Anonymous

"Life is too short not to be exhilarated every moment or reveling in your pain."—Melodie D. Tucker

Passion

Guiding others to discover what they really want out of life and helping them figure out how to get it is my life's passion. Whether it is creating a loving, long-lasting relationship, a happy, healthy family life, a fulfilling, successful career or all of the above (and more!), it is my privilege as a Mars Venus Success Coach to help people achieve their dreams.

I've also recently rediscovered my artistic talent for crafting beautiful paintings. After a 25-year hiatus, I'm once again pouring my heart and emotions onto the canvas. It transports me to another dimension and dissolves stress and sorrow.

Darkest Hour

In June 2002, my 67-year old mother, stepdad and 12-year old adopted brother traveled to Florida for a two-week visit. My mother became too ill to travel back north. Although we both had full-time careers at Kennedy Space Center, my compassionate husband and I quickly regrouped and made room for them to live with us indefinitely. Within a few weeks, the doctor prescribed oxygen, a wheelchair and did surgery to implant a chest port so no more needles would bruise her arms. Before she left the hospital, he authorized Hospice to assist us at my home. Hospital bed, potty chair, shower chair, wheelchair, oxygen machine, portable tanks and a myriad assortment of other daily necessities arrived.

We had good days and bad days. One July afternoon, we set up the video recorder and I prompted my mother with open-ended questions designed to inspire storytelling. As she talked, I sat with her and held her hand.

She had survived breast cancer six years before, yet the radiation therapy had caused myelodysplasia disorder, a leukemia-like disease that is battled with blood transfusions or even bone marrow transplants if one is young and healthy enough. The specialist we visited in September determined she was already too frail to be a candidate.

In October, my youngest daughter (who was born with cerebral palsy) had her third knee surgery, with a fourth scheduled for after the first of the year.

In November, my husband began to complain about pain in his right side. Thinking it was gall bladder trouble, he went to the doctor in December, but the bleak news was that he had renal cell carcinoma in his left kidney and it would have to be removed ASAP. Fear drenched me like hot glue. I couldn't imagine losing both my dear mother and my wonderful husband *at the same time.*

January 6 began my mother's final week. My daughter had her scheduled knee surgery two days later. My mother's fevers raged and each day she descended further. Friday she received her final transfusion, but it did no good.

That Saturday morning, she died peacefully in my home at the exact time of my eldest daughter's 24th birthday at 11:25 a.m. We all knew how much holiday and birthday traditions had meant to my mother. This miracle was the only gift she could bestow on her very first and precious grandchild that year, but it's surely one that will last a lifetime.

Her funeral was January 16, and two weeks later it was time for my husband's kidney cancer surgery. His two sisters, his mom, our two daughters and I were all there when the doctor came in to report that it was over and no other cancer was found. I couldn't wait to tell him!

The next morning he was groggily coming around at 9:15 on February 1, 2003, as I watched out of his 7th floor Cape Canaveral Hospital window, awaiting the arrival of the Space Shuttle Columbia. It never made it home, but instead disintegrated over Texas.

Lessons from the Dark

If it weren't for the darkness, how would we appreciate the light? Darkness is, if not good, still a necessary and natural part of this life. It is a small price to pay for the gift of emotion. So when storm clouds gather, learning to remain positive and finding joy in the simple things can serve to make each and every day special, no matter what drama swirls around us. Letting go and letting God – or Goddess, whichever you prefer – teaches that the only thing we have control over is our own behavior, attitude, reactions or responses. Empower yourself by seeking the positives in any situation.

Brightest Hour

My husband and I have adventured over 32 years together, on planes, trains, ships and buses as well as in a motor home, a travel trailer, two pop-up campers, four tents, four vans and nine family automobiles, including a leaky T-Top Cutlass Supreme and a Durango Copper Pearl Mid-Life Crisis Dream Machine. We've traveled from the Space Center to Santa Maria, Santa Barbara, Santa Margarita, San Luis to San Simeon to San Francisco; Seattle to Santa Fe to Silverton to Salt Lake City to St. Louis to Salem; Custer to Canada to Cincinnati to Chatsworth, Cozumel, Costa Rica, and Key West.

We've raised two kids, four dogs, eight cats, some kittens, some goldfish, six hamsters and two cockatiels. We've battled lice, ticks, termites, fleas, roaches, rats, snakes, spiders, scorpions, viruses and bacteria galore.

We juggled our aerospace careers between piano, voice, violin, baton, dance, acting, swimming and horseback riding lessons and Girl Scouts and Brownies and ball practice and swim meets and parades, appointments, summer camps and science projects as well as the routine house chores, shopping, cooking, laundry and yard work.

We've clapped endlessly through orchestra (yes, Mississippi Hot Dog IS still Twinkle, Twinkle Little Star), chorus, piano and dance recitals, swim meets, softball games, award ceremonies, plays, musicals, and science fairs. We've wheeled-and-dealed with teachers, administrators, principles, counselors, doctors, dentists, nurses, county, state and federal bureaucrats of all kinds.

We've dwelled together in one apartment, one duplex, one timeshare, three condos, three houses and six eternally long nights in the Wuesthoff Pediatric Ward beside our youngest daughter, who at 14 had just survived a 10-hour back surgery. We dabbled with a rental property and a lot full of citrus trees. We've camped without electricity or running water and languished at the Trump Plaza – all in the same week! We've luxuriated at the finest hotels atop Las Vegas and San Francisco and feared bedbugs from the Friendship Motel. And we've bobbed on The Emerald Seas, The Tropicale, The Fantasy and The Jubilee.

We've gazed at the campfire and starlight in Yosemite, the Redwoods, the Rockies, The Smokies, Lake Tahoe, Burne Caverns, The Grand Canyon, The Black Hills, Yellowstone and Bryce Canyon. We've roasted at Niagara Falls and frozen in Valencia.

We've weathered hurricanes (and 'him'icanes), lightning strikes, fire and floods. We've navigated through panic attacks, depression, cerebral palsy, impacted wisdom teeth, heart problems, menopause, scoliosis, staph infections, surgeries, pneumonia, chicken pox, cancer, car accidents and illnesses with no name.

But there's been no famine – I've created fantastic feasts, marvelous meals, salty suppers, funky fare, breakfast buffets, spicy spreads, sweet smorgasbords and simple snacks.

All the while he fixed faucets and fans and furniture and Fords and fuel filters and five million other things on the list! We've remodeled and redone and painted and nailed and sawed and stripped and sanded and stained.

There have been so many "Diamond Days." Our wedding day, our first anniversary all alone in a Hayes Kansas campground, the birth of our babies, a stand of Pines in California when the cops caught us "necking" in the car on our 10th anniversary. And some of those wild and magical days, nights and weekends...only *he* knows which ones I mean.

And so many holidays and parties! Yuletide Lasagna, Halloween Horrors and Humors, Easter Feasts, Valentine's Romance, Birthday Bashes, BBQs & Picnics for the Fourth and Labor Day and Memorial Day, and Carol-a-longs and So-Longs.

All the little carnivals, the County Fairs, the State Fairs, the Renaissance Faires, Disney Land, Disney World, Sea World, Busch Gardens, Cypress Gardens, Silver Springs, Salt Springs, Juniper Springs, Blue Springs, Wild Waters, Wet & Wild, Six Flags, Magic Mountain, Williamsburg, Monticello, Biltmore, Hearst Castle, Summer by the Sea, Winter in Tahoe, Spring in the Desert, and Autumn EVERYWHERE!

Lessons from the Light

Family and friends are so precious and dear
Those from far and those from near
Who have mirrored our smiles and shared our tears
Through the fun as well as the fears
Those who've meant so very much throughout the years.

There is no place like home...and that is wherever my husband happens to be. I am his "Lady" and I loved him then, I love him now and I will love him until death do us part. It is ONE MARRIAGE.

Biography

Melodie D. Tucker is a Mars Venus Success Coach, seminar facilitator and public speaker. She's presented on cruise ships, at churches and resorts and for professional women's organizations and conferences. She authors many articles for Mars Venus and currently is a featured monthly columnist for familiesonlinemagazine.com. She is also a trainer and recruiter for Mars Venus coaches worldwide.

In 2005, Melodie retired from a 30-plus year career in the aerospace industry at Kennedy Space Center, with 17 years as a manager. She enjoys oil painting, as well as travel, camping and billiards with her husband of 32 years, Charles Tucker, a retired NASA manager. They reside in Merritt Island, Fla. and have two adult daughters.

Melodie D. Tucker

melodietucker@marsvenuscoaching.com
www.marsvenuscoaching.com/tucker
321-459-1399

Chapter Twenty-Three

Linda Wiggins

Favorite Quote

"Banish Doubt: Only your dream is real." I wrote it. It is so true. There is so much negativity in the world, but the only way I can be derailed from what I really have a passion to accomplish is if I make fear "realer" than my dream.

Passion

It has been my passion and my dream to help women who have achieved a degree of professional success find lifelong happiness with a man. It seems so common that these skills are mutually exclusive. I initially thought for my life's darkest hour I would write about how I earned my theme *Being Mrs. Right: It's not about Finding Mr. Right, but First Being Mrs. Right*, a blog and book in progress. Then I realized that after two-plus years of financial assault, my marriage was on the rocks and I didn't have a paddle. I had to help myself before I could again help anyone else.

Darkest Hour

My husband and I looked at home movies from Christmas morning from five years ago and I almost didn't recognize myself. I was confident, capable of commanding deep love from my husband simply by not needing it. It was a certain *je ne sais quoi*, something I couldn't put my finger on, but I was on top of my game.

We had gone into business shortly after my daughter was born, and what a thrill. The business was wildly successful, and though we paid quite a lot for it resale, the value skyrocketed as open territories for the franchise were snapped up. I partnered with an emotionally frail family member in a relationship peppered with land mines, and when she proposed I buy her out so she could indulge her wanderlust, I jumped at the chance to be free. Yes, I was also motivated in part by the chance to have 100 percent control of the decision-making and all of the profits. Financing fell through and I should have walked away from the deal, but I caved in to her legal threats and badgered my husband until he agreed to use the equity in our home to finance the buyout.

What should have accomplished the end of acrid relations was only the beginning of more excruciating ugliness between my former business partner and me. Business fell off and I felt like a failure. It was hell going in to work every day, painting enthusiasm on a face of dread. There is nothing like seeing a business die a little more every day, and to see your money vanish more quickly than the cavalry of resale or economic recovery can arrive. We had used up all our home equity in what the nation discovered was a huge bubble, which then burst. We dipped into our 401K and IRAs until we were practically wiped out before we threw in the towel. We would either have to close both businesses or – and this option was awful but the most fair to my creditors – call in my former partner to take over in exchange for debts to everyone but ourselves. At least the blood loss would be through, and we could focus our efforts on our home foreclosure and bankruptcy, our once stellar credit rating now destroyed. We called my former partner and simply "let it go."

I discovered that financial security ranked high on my husband's list of priorities, and with our home and savings gone, he was a mess. And like Adam before him, he blamed his woman and God for the outcome of the choices he made.

For two-plus years I second-guessed my business decisions with the brilliance of hindsight, my feet madly dancing to Mike's bullets of blame. I tied up the loose ends of the business and started the search for a job where I could make as much money as possible so that I could "fix my mistakes" and try to save our house. Never mind that it would mean precious little time to spend with my children. Suddenly I realized I didn't know what I was talking about. I was no Mrs. Right. I could no longer conduct myself in a manner that made my man feel like he was the luckiest guy on the planet and treat me accordingly. I took a stand with my husband and found a job where I could make reasonable money and not have to work crazy hours. I then sent Mrs. Right back to remedial level so I could benefit from this tragedy through lessons learned from this dark hour.

Lessons from the Dark

I see now that God puts us where he needs us, and if we go along with the plan, we can be of great help to others. Now that legions of fellow Americans have joined us in the foreclosure and bankruptcy nightmare, I no longer feel like a failure. We were simply the first ones to get hit by the train.

We have already been through the house of horrors and we can tell others just going in that everything will be OK. I learned that a savings account, a strong economy, our home equity, none of those things is my sufficiency, God is. He is the Source of all provisions and will always provide for my need.

Brightest Hour

This is the evolution of Mrs. Right: My dating "career" got off on the right track at age 14. Larry was crazy about me and I really barely noticed him. This despite the fact he was friends with my sisters who are nearly three years older than me, an otherwise perfect recipe for coveting a guy my 17-year-old sisters thought was dreamy. Somehow along the way, I decided his bad-boy best friend was a much better choice, and it was downhill from then on until I got my head right about a decade ago. Could it be 20 years of bad karma from such a despicable act?

I overcame great obstacles to complete higher education and land jobs as a newspaper reporter, my absolute dream. This from a Detroit native whose greatest hope would have been to land a job in an auto plant and retire to start living after 30 years, except there was no hope for that path by the time I came along. My dating career left a lot of ruin in its wake, mostly repeat destruction of my own heart as I subjected myself to inevitable rejection by: being the first to spark up a conversation (maybe he's The One and if I don't say something the chance will be lost!), pursuing the guy (he's just shy, or needs help getting over "that witch" so he can love me), sleeping with him too soon (auditioning for a role, giving away free samples), allowing myself to be more in love with him than he was with me, pressing him for more than he was ready to feel (the ultimate kiss of death in a relationship), all to satisfy my unquenchable insecurity. In terms of self-esteem, I grew to feel lower than a snake's belly in a wagon's rut. Through research into endless self-help books I learned so many things about what I was doing wrong, but for many years I refused to change my approach. It really was painful waiting for the man to pursue me; it required a lot of faith that I didn't yet have. Finally, the pain of continuing to hurt myself became greater than the pain of change.

Literally, the moment I let go of the last relationship I had trashed by doing things my old way and committed to doing things God's way no matter what, the next man I met pursued me through marriage and two children. I finally have my other dream, the dream of a family of my own.

My children are my life's greatest blessings and I am crazy in love with them. I'm not crazy in love with my husband and I never will be, thank you God; I won't love him more than he loves me. Loving Mike doesn't hurt, like my old definition of love. It makes me feel good about myself. Life is full of paradoxes, and in a paradox is buried great truth. When I quit pursing a man to try to get him to love me so that I could feel good about myself, a man could love me. I had to love myself enough to wait for a man to pursue me, and now I feel good about myself.

Lessons from the Light

I learned that a man cannot meet my needs by reading my mind. I have to ask for a man's help in a sweet way, containing not a trace of resentment, and then acknowledge him profusely for it – even if it is merely taking out the garbage, or some other task I may feel he ought naturally do. When this happens, the man is fulfilled in life and looks for more ways to please me, because pleasing me makes him feel so good. I have to give credit to Dr. John Gray, author of the *Men are from Mars, Women are from Venus* series. Of all the many books I've read, *Mars and Venus on a Date* is the one that contained God's how-to of finding a husband, and when I recently became aware I'd fallen off that path, *Mars and Venus Together Forever* helped me find it again.

What I learned recently that put me back on track is that somehow in my darkest hour I'd fallen into my old pattern of accepting bad treatment from a man and then trying to "fix it" so he would love me. I accepted Mike's blame and scrambled to make as much money as I could to "fix it," and was willing to let it cost me my time with my children – the absolute best gift God has ever given me. When I saw this, I stopped in my tracks and the next time and each time it happened I said, "I feel blamed and I don't want that." Through this simple awareness and simple act, I was able to release my resentment and get back to doing the things that make a successful wife Mrs. Right, among them, asking for what I needed in a sweet way and fulfilling him by my appreciation of his efforts. In turn, I become fulfilled to overflowing and love spills out over the top.

The price of a great relationship is eternal vigilance. Wait. Maybe *that's* my favorite quote.

Biography

Linda Wiggins is a writer and writing coach living in Melbourne, Fla. with her husband, daughter and son. After many years as a reporter and columnist across the globe, she considers her toughest challenge and greatest achievement becoming *Mrs. Right*.

Linda Wiggins

P.O. Box 411411
Melbourne, FL 32941-1411
www.beingmrsright.com
LindaWiggins123@aol.com

Foundational Elements of Positive Psychology by Dr. Wanda Bethea

This project was a creative victory. Writing about my darkest and brightest hours was a chance for me to remember, heal and smile. I forced myself to return to the dark place and bring it to light. In psychological theory, "regression in the service of the ego," is the premise that you can only heal from painful past events if you recall or go back to them with a broader and deeper understanding. Anyone who has ever been in psychotherapy may understand this when your therapist "reframed" and "relabeled" your negative early life events in order to get you to move beyond the pain.

Writing about the lessons I learned from living through the darkest and brightest hours most definitely speaks to my sense of gratitude. This character strength and others such as spirituality, fairness, love of learning, wisdom, zest and curiosity have served me well in my personal and professional life. The opportunity to put these lessons on paper was a blessing. This project was brought to me and that felt like a divine plan. I hope by sharing the following foundational elements of Positive Psychology that it will help you find your character strengths and lead a more vibrant life.

Vibrant Women's Wisdom is an invitation to you to witness the power of strengths in action. Positive Psychology is the scientific study of how people can experience well-being and "authentic" happiness by using their strengths every day in work, love, play and parenting.* I was honored to be among the women in this book who used their strengths to learn lessons, count their blessings and enhance their vibrancy for life. As a psychologist who promoted Positive Psychology principles for years, I am excited to be part of a project wherein people wrote their stories showing how they used various strengths (wisdom, courage, humanity, forgiveness, leadership and humor) in order to survive dark hours and thrive in bright ones.

Martin Seligman and Chris Peterson, the early Positive Psychology researchers, classified 24 character strengths grouped under six categories or core values (Wisdom & Knowledge, Courage, Humanity & Love, Justice, Temperance and Transcendence).

Wisdom and Knowledge
1. Curiosity – Being open to new ideas and experiences.
2. Creativity – Discovering and expressing original ideas, not limited to artistic works.
3. Open Mindedness – Thinking things through, examining them from all sides, not jumping to conclusions.
4. Love of Learning – Having an enthusiasm for learning new ideas and skills.
5. Perspective/Wisdom – Being able to look at world in a way that makes sense to others and yourself; Helping others solve problems and gain perspective.

Courage
6. Bravery – Taking action in spite of dangers or unpopular outcomes.
7. Persistence – Striving for a goal despite obstacles and setbacks; Taking on tough projects and finishing them without being obsessive or perfectionist.
8. Honesty – Speaking the truth and presenting you in an honest way.
9. Zest – Living life with vitality, enthusiasm – as an adventure.

Humanity and Love
10. Love – Loving yourself and others in more than a romantic way; Being loved.
11. Kindness – Caring and "being compassion" without the expectation of personal gain.
12. Social/Personal & Emotional Intelligence – "Being awareness" of your own and others' emotions and intentions; Responding well to others; Putting yourself where your skills, abilities and relationships are readily affirmed and validated.

Justice
13. Teamwork – Working as a member of a group for the common good.
14. Fairness – Treating people according to ideals of equality and justice.
15. Leadership – Motivating and coordinating a group of people to achieve a common goal.

Temperance

16. Forgiveness & Mercy – Forgiving those who have wronged or offended you.
17. Modesty – Allowing your strengths and accomplishments to speak for themselves without the need to brag about them.
18. Prudence – Being careful about your choices
19. Self-Regulation – Exerting control over you in order to achieve goals and meet standards.

Transcendence

20. Appreciation of Beauty and Excellence – Feeling a sense of awe and wonder in responses to beautiful things.
21. Gratitude – Being thankful for the good things in your life.
22. Optimism – Expecting good things to happen in the future.
23. Humor – Enjoying laughter, friendly teasing and being playful.
24. Spirituality – Having knowledge of your place within the larger scheme of things. Having a sense of the sacred.

*FOOTNOTE: Quoted from *Authentic Happiness*, Martin Seligman, 2002. Seligman is referred to as the "Father of Positive Psychology." Chris Peterson and Martin Seligman studied religions and philosophers across historical periods and different cultures and proposed a classification of 24 character strengths. To take their free online character strengths questionnaire, VIA (Values-in-Action), go to www.authentichappiness.org.

In *Vibrant Women's Wisdom*, each author noticeably demonstrated one or more of these character strengths as she experienced divorce, death of a loved one, major relocations and other transitions. Each woman endures, "tangles on," is still standing to tell her stories and is thriving despite the traumas and turmoil. Now, that's the epitome of resilience or "bounceback," which is about using negative experiences as a springboard that inspires future achievement and success.**

The power of using your strengths daily in various areas of your life (work, love, play and parenting) is exponential. You enhance your well-being, life satisfaction, goal setting, immune system and relationships as you discover and apply your strengths daily. The key point is, Positive Psychology focuses more on what is right with you and best in you, rather than on what is wrong with you or mediocre in you. *Vibrant Women's Wisdom* is all about dark hours that did not block the bright hours, lessons (sometimes called "blessings") and character strengths.

We invite you to complete the worksheets/activities at the end of this book. (APPENDICES) You, therefore, will write/journal about your darkest and brightest hours. By doing so, you can reveal the lessons you learned and identify the salient strengths you possess. You might form a journal group with friends or strangers with whom you share and compare your hours.

There also are opportunities for you to add your favorite quotations. These work sheets might be the beginning of your own book. Who knows what might evolve? I wish for you wisdom and knowledge, courage, humanity and love, justice, temperance and transcendence.

** FOOTNOTE: Quoted from *Average to A+ Realising Strengths in Yourself and Others*, Alex Linley, 2008. To use Linley's comprehensive strengths identification and development tool, Realise2, go to www.realise2.org

Positive Psychology: Foundational Self-Research

Identify and list five strengths you remember using during childhood. Maybe those strengths were used more when you were at home, in school, in sports in a community center or somewhere else. Who were you with? What were you doing? How did you feel?

Then, indicate in what area of your life (home, school, hobby, etc.) you used that particular strength. If you still have contact with anyone who knew you then (if you feel comfortable), ask that person to tell you what she/he remembers about you. That is another way to access your strengths during childhood.

Identify and list five strengths you remember using during adolescence. Maybe those strengths were used more at home, in school, in sports, in a community center or somewhere else. Who were you with? What were you doing? How did you feel?

Then, indicate in what area of your life (home, school, hobby, etc.) you used that particular strength. If you still have contact with anyone who knew you then (if you feel comfortable), ask that person to tell you what she/he observed about your strengths during adolescence.

Identify the darkest hour of your life. Start writing and do not edit for spelling, grammar or logical content. Just write. You might only write one or two sentences a day for seven days. You may not be able to write more than a sentence a week. Just begin the process. What happened? Who was there? Why were they there? How did you feel? Did someone hurt and abandon you? Or did someone do or not do something that made it the darkest hour?

CAUTION: If any of these suggestions regarding how to gather your information about the darkest hour are NOT helpful, then follow your own path. These are YOUR stories.

Lessons Learned from My Darkest Hour

Identify the brightest hour of your life. Start writing and do not edit for spelling, grammar or logical content. Just write. You might only write one or two sentences a day for seven days. You may not be able to write more than a sentence a week. Just begin the process. What happened? Who was there? Why were they there? How did you feel? Did someone support and encourage you? Or did someone do or not do something that made it the brightest hour?

CAUTION: If any of these suggestions regarding how to gather your information about the brightes hour are NOT helpful, then follow your own path. These are YOUR stories.

Lessons Learned from My Brightest Hour

Writing Your Own Vibrant Women's Wisdom Story

By Linda Wiggins, Writing Coach

Many of us have availed ourselves of valuable tools through our journey through darkness to light. Personally, Dr. Wanda Bethea has been a touchtone through my journey, ever available to me through this process over the phone or in person to help me neutralize the negative emotions that get me "hooked," so that I can get back on my right path toward The Light. We as women are more apt than men to reach out for emotional support, but I know in my experience I can choose to stay in pain longer than I need to before I am forced to reach out for help. My recommendation to you is that you reach out, to a trusted girlfriend or girlfriends, to a life coach, to a licensed professional, or all of the above, but reach out.

Once you have used Dr. Wanda's valuable tools to delve into your past and present experiences, you may want use this valuable "research" to write your own Vibrant Women's Wisdom story of Surviving & Thriving Through Dark and Bright Hours. The following is a workbook format that you can write into directly, or better, you can retype into your own computer. You may also go to www.VibrantWomensWisdom.com to download the format and access many other helpful tools.

Be aware that as you start this process, you may encounter feelings of discomfort, anger, sadness or a general malaise you cannot put your finger on. In trying to figure out what the problem is, you will be tempted to make a problem out of the problem. Drama. The darkness in you wants to stay in the dark. Dark hates The Light. It does not want you to be healthy and whole, because then you will be available for a deeper relationship with The Light, and available to be of help to others in deepening their relationship with The Light.

Push on. Write on. The rewards are well worth it.

Write your chapter:

Name:

Favorite Quote (50 words or less):

Passion (100 words or less):

Your chapter continued:

Darkest Hour (500 words or less):

Lessons from the Dark (100 words or less):

Your chapter continued:

Brightest Hour (500 words or less):

Lessons from the Light (100 words or less):

Your chapter continued:

Your Biography (120 words or less):

There are Only Dark Hours for Victims of Human Trafficking

Some of the proceeds from this book go to end Human Trafficking through the women's organization Zonta International. Kelly Palace is a passionate supporter of this organization, as is contributing author Claire Ellis who is President of the Melbourne, Florida Zonta Chapter.

Human trafficking is rampant in the world today. It is estimated that between 600,000 and 800,000 victims are trafficked across international borders each year. It is a $9-$17 billion international industry, second only to drug trafficking. Eighty percent of the victims are female and half are children.

Cases of human trafficking have been reported in all 50 states, Washington D.C. and some U.S. territories. Victims of human trafficking can be children or adults, U.S. citizens or foreign nationals, male or female. An estimated 15,000-18,000 victims are trafficked annually into the United States. At any given time there are 43,000 trafficked victims in the U.S. Here is a harrowing statistic: only 2 percent are rescued.

Zonta clubs are being asked to collaborate with local governments, non-governmental organizations, community leaders, the media, law enforcement agencies, and the general public to eliminate trafficking in persons, especially women and girls, through the three P's strategy.

- PREVENT conditions driving demand and supply for trafficking, illegal prostitution and sexual exploitation.
- PROTECT trafficking victims by providing reintegration assistance and opportunities for social inclusion.
- PROSECUTE and punish traffickers. Criminalize all forms of trafficking.

You can help us implement the "three P's" for this worthy cause. For more information visit www.zonta.org.

Please visit our website:
www.VibrantWomensWisdom.com